# A Man of

# Significance

Doris Gaines Rapp, Ph.D.

# A Man of Significance

Daniel's House Publishing - Huntington, Indiana

In cooperation with Never Alone Publishing
Fort Wayne, Indiana

Copyright 2023 Doris Gaines Rapp

This personality sketch is based on genealogical research. Because the events occurred in the 1500s and 1600s, it is possible that some data may be incorrect.

All rights reserved. No part of this publication may be reproduced or transmitted in any form or by any electronic or mechanical means including photocopying, recording, or any information storage and retrieval system now known or to be invented, without permission in writing from the publisher or the author.

Name: Doris Gaines Rapp, Ph.D.

Title: A Man of Significance – Personality Sketch, Narrative Nonfiction

Identifiers: LCCN: 2023911172

ISBN: 978-1-7365110-9-1 (paperback)

ISBN: 979-8-9885283-0-2 (eBook)

Cover Design: Debi Lindhorst – The Type Galley, Warren, Indiana

Cover image: A Vector illustration of an old black man with pipe. Shutterstock: Stock Vector ID: 2181687819

All Scripture quotations, unless otherwise indicated, are taken from the Holy Bible, New International Version®, NIV®. Copyright ©1973, 1978, 1984, 2011 by Biblica, Inc.™ Used by permission of Zondervan. All rights reserved worldwide. www.zondervan.com The "NIV" and "New International Version" are trademarks registered in the United States Patent and Trademark Office by Biblica, Inc.™

Published by Daniel's House Publishing - Huntington, Indiana
in cooperation with Never Alone Publishing - Fort Wayne, Indiana

Daniel's House Publishing - Huntington, Indiana

In cooperation with Never Alone Publishing - Fort Wayne, Indiana

## Acknowledgements

Isaac Barber, in the Office of Student Success at Huntington, Indiana, I so appreciate your enthusiasm in reading some chapters of *A Man of Significance* to help with wording. The students at Huntington are lucky you are there for them.

Ted Frantz, Ph.D. Chair of the History and Political Science Department at the University of Indianapolis, deserves a big thank you as well. Another voice to ensure the correct use of words and terms was valuable to me. Thanks for the book recommendation. *All That She Carried* is wonderful.

I want to thank Kim Autrey, editor at Never Alone Publishing, for all of your consistent work. You are so helpful and positive I continue to be uplifted by your enthusiasm and expertise. Thanks Kim.

A big thank you to Vicki Borgman who is always faithful in reading my books. She gives great suggestions, and sometimes finds that occasional missing comma or repetition.

Thanks to Donna Nehring who has begun reading my books as well. After reading the manuscript many, many times, I fail to see when I'm repeating myself. Fresh eyes are appreciated.

Thanks to Debi Lindhorst at the Type Galley in Warren, Indiana. You do wonders with computer work way beyond my guess-and-miss form of cover and picture creating.

# Man of Significance

**Table of Contents**

| Page | Chapter | |
|---|---|---|
| 15 | 1 | Grandpa John |
| 24 | 2 | The Universal Family |
| 32 | 3 | Blessed |
| 38 | | Map of Africa |
| 36 | 4 | The New World |
| 41 | 5 | Who are Your People? |
| 48 | 6 | The Land of Ndongo |
| 53 | 7 | The Land Your Early Family Called Home |
| 57 | 8 | John Gowen's Homeland |
| 64 | 9 | Your Search for Your Ancestor's Homeland |
| 68 | 10 | Social Structure |
| 71 | 11 | Slave History in Your Ancestor's Country-of-Origin |
| 73 | 12 | Portugal's Attempts at Colonization |
| 79 | 13 | Religion of Angola |
| 84 | 14 | Portuguese Influence and Power |
| 89 | 15 | The Shaping of Your Ancestor's Country |
| 91 | 16 | Foods of Angola |
| 97 | 17 | Foods from Your Ancestor's Home of Origin |
| 99 | 18 | Clothing of Ndongo |
| 108 | 19 | The Traditional Clothing of Your Country |

| 110 | 20 | Family |
| 115 | 21 | Family Life in Your Ancestor's Home |
| 117 | 22 | Girls |
| 120 | 23 | Courting Practices |
| 122 | 24 | Villages and Language |
| 125 | 25 | Your Family's Language |
| 128 | 26 | Growth and Development of the Virginia Colony |
| 136 | 27 | Growth of Your Ancestor's Homeland |
| 138 | 28 | Freedom |
| 147 | 29 | Event(s) in the Life of Your Lost One |
| 149 | 30 | Second Generation: Mihill (Michael) Gowen, Son of John Gowen |
| 154 | 31 | Third Generation: Thomas Christopher Gowen |
| 156 | 32 | A Little History of Jamestown Nearby Neighbors |
| 164 | 33 | Points of Historic Interest in Your Ancestor's Country |
| 166 | 34 | Slave Law |
| 170 | 35 | Blessed |
| 173 | 36 | Are You Blessed? |
| 175 | 37 | A Man of Significance |
| 186 | 38 | Your Own Significant Relative |

## Illustrations and Photo

Page 16. Fig. 1 A Vector illustration of an old black man with smoking pipe. Shutterstock: Stock Vector ID: 2181687819

Page 21. Fig. 2 Author, Doris Gaines Rapp. Pasadena Grade School. Kettering, Ohio - Age 6

Page 35. Fig. 3 Africa. Creative Fabrica - Africa map by ingoFonts/Ingo Zimmerman

Page 37. Fig. 4 Landing of the *White Lion* at Jamestown. Shutterstock ID: 237228061

Page 49. Fig. 5 Ndongo (Angola). Image ID 1910276290 Shutterstock

Page 50. Fig. 6 Slaves in Africa Image ID 237236935 Shutterstock

Page 58. Fig.7 Red-Tailed Monkey Shutterstock ID 1258276933

Page 59. Fig. 8 Aardvark ID 18990396 Shutterstock

Page 59. Fig. 9 Cape Buffalo Shutterstock ID 727249078

Page 60. Fig.10 Giant Sable Antelope ID 2186798977

Page 102. Fig. 11 Queen Njinga meeting with Portuguese Governor Joao Corria de Sousa, 1622 Public Domain image

Page 104. Fig. 12. Historic Williamsburg reenactor. Taken

April 2023. Doris Gaines Rapp

Page 105. Fig, 13. Leather breeches. Photo – Williamsburg, VA. Doris Gaines Rapp

Page 106. Fig. 14. Right of left shoe from cobbler, Williamsburg. Doris Gaines Rapp

Page 107. Fig. 15. Cobbler's Bench and tools. Doris Gaines Rapp

Page 113. Fig. 16. Chicken photo. Contributed by Rachel Marie Hester.

Page 113. Fig. 17. Lamb. Contributed by Rachel Marie Hester.

Page 128. Fig. 18. Jamestown Settlement 1619. Image ID 1353146165 Shutterstock.

Page 129. Fig. 19. James River, Virginia. Taken April 2023. Doris Gaines Rapp

Page 130. Fig. 20. Jamestown Fort Meeting House. Taken April 2023. Doris Gaines Rapp.

Page 131. Fig. 21. Mud and Stud construction. Photo taken April 2023. Doris Gaines Rapp

Page 131. Fig. 22. Stick Framing. Jamestown Settlement. Photo - April 2023. Doris Gaines Rapp

Page 132. Fig. 23. Inside Governor Delaware's house, Jamestown Settlement. Photo – Doris Gaines Rapp.

Page 132. Fig. 24. Ibid.

Page 140. Fig. 25. Sailing ship. Jamestown Settlement. Photo – Doris Gaines Rapp

Page 156. Fig. 26. Native American Dwelling, near Jamestown Settlement – Doris Gaines Rapp

Page 159. Fig. 27. Captain. John Smith statue – Jamestown Historic Settlement – Bill Rapp

Page 160. Fig. 28. Musket firing at Jamestown Settlement. Photo – Doris Gaines Rapp

Page 162. Fig. 29. Remains of church chancel – Historic Jamestown. Photo April 2023. Doris Gaines Rapp

Page 162. Fig. 30. Statue of Pocahontas in Historic Jamestown. Photo April 2023. Doris Gaines Rapp

Page 176. Fog. 31. Planted tobacco in mounts – Jamestown Settlement. Doris Gaines Rapp

Page 186. Fig. 32. Shutterstock ID 1718280706. Nail Cross Christian Nail Cross Vector Illustrator Lettering added and Trademarked.

In loving memory of all those who went before us,
those we know, and those who remain in the fog of time.
When we can call our distant grandparents
by their name, they become real,
and a significant part of our family

# Chapter One

## Grandpa John

Has the bubble you live in ever expanded so fast you could hear it pop? Mine has. Like other children, my safe world consisted of my family. My mother's parents were only an hour away, and Daddy's nieces and nephews were my best friends. As an adult, my sister, Donna, stretched the circumference of my world by stuffing it with genealogy research. She was able to include the names of some of our distant relatives in our family tree. But when I took the Ancestry DNA test, my world burst wide open. I was shocked and confused. How could I have an ancestor so different from what I have always known as family? I was captivated by him and had to learn more.

My fifth great-grandfather, born in 1660, was Thomas Christopher "Sobering Wind" Gowen: black, white, and part Cherokee. His wife, my fifth great-grandmother, born in 1656, was Winona Dakota WinuNna, Cherokee Indian.

What? Several years ago, the paper trail I followed led our Gaines line, my dad's side of the family, back to England and the knights of old. There was something about a man named Gams, meaning a squint eye, whom the king knighted for bravery of some sort. I wasn't even close. Sobering Wind?

Ancestry.com said our Gaines line came to America before the Pilgrims landed at Plymouth Rock. I was stunned. As they say, DNA doesn't lie. According to Thomas Christopher Gowen's linage, his grandfather, my seventh great-grandfather, John Gowen came to the Virginia Colony in 1619 on the *White Lion* from Ndongo, now Angola, Africa, on the first "slave-ship" bound for North America. I had to know these people ... my people.

*Fig. 1 Black Man with Pipe*

Since I don't know very much about those distance relatives, I am often stumped for words to express my feelings. Unlike Tiya Miles in her wonderfully expressive book, *All That She Carried,* I don't have family stories to tell you about. Only the few records I could find.

In those documents, you will find the name, Gowen, spelled many ways in the quoted sections of the book (John Graweere/Geaween/Gowen/Goin). If you'll notice, there are also many misspelled words in the quoted historic portions. I'll spell his name Gowen.

Thomas Christopher's father, Mihill (Michael), was born on Lt. Robert Sheppard's Plantation to John Gowen and Margaret Cornish. Lt. Sheppard was named Mihill's godfather at the time of the infant's Christening.

Researching for this book, there are arguments on both sides regarding John and Margaret's marriage. I am here, so my ancestors were someone ... and many. I choose to follow the paper trail to Thomas Gowen, my fifth great-grandfather according to my DNA.

As a psychologist, educator, and fiction author, the importance to me was not just their names. The challenge became, what would I do about the breathtaking information?

• • •

When I was growing up, every family gathering at our house was a party. Some of the cousins and I played croquet in the side yard beyond the fluffy balls of the peony bushes, where the sweet aroma from the roses on the trellis mingled with the huge pink blossoms. My sister and older cousins usually huddled upstairs in Donna's room to discuss the cutest boy in school or other exciting bits and pieces of a teenager's life. Mama and the aunts sat on the glider and side chairs on the front porch and chattered while the bluebirds sang. Daddy and the uncles enjoyed the day in the backyard near the yucca plants as they putted a few golf balls or watched the grass grow. We were all close. Family was everything. My whole family consisted of that wonderful first generation of loved ones.

Much later, like many of you, I became fascinated with finding my great-great-grandparents. My maternal grandmother told me a little about her parents and grandparents, mostly Northern European. But my Norwegian grandfather was an introvert who talked very little about everything. His side of the family was a blur of sketchy statements. Who else didn't I know? Who were the people from the foggy past? What surprises waited for me?

I'm not a historian. It would take far more years of study, more research, and more expertise in the field of Historiography than I have to fully research my extended family. My DNA found the names for me, revealing ninety of my fifth great-grandparents alone.

I'm a psychologist. I'm interested in individual people and how they come to do the things they do. In individual sessions, I often counsel in parables. Most of my books are fiction as an author, and I'm still wrapping events with words and descriptions. The story of people's lives and loves and living circumstances are the things that draw me to them.

Before her death, Phoebe Jane Bryson, my grandfather's mother, lived on the farm with Grandma and Grandpa. As a two or three-year-old child, I remember great-grandma in a long black dress, sitting in her dark oak rocking chair with the brown leather seat in the farmhouse gathering room. She, too, didn't say much, and I kept my distance. Think of the painting of *Whistler's Mother*, and you will know a little about how she looked. Great-grandma ate her peas with a knife, which, even as a toddler, I realized how silly and impossible that would be. I never tried it myself. I had enough trouble keeping my vegetables on a spoon without complicating the culinary issue.

Mother dropped little snippets of information about my Scandinavian and Scottish distant family from time to time, but only as part of other conversations. One evening while I sat at the dining room table practicing my cursive letters, Mother said, "My Uncle James had beautiful handwriting. His writing was so neat: he addressed the Christmas cards for the president of the New York Central Railroad," or some large company that now slips my mind. Mother expanded on my great-uncle's talents in calligraphy by adding: "Those cards went to President Roosevelt, the King and Queen of England, and other dignitaries." Looking at my own less-than-artful handwriting, I was impressed.

But my father's side of the family was littered with blanks and fuzzy spots. Daddy's mother died at forty-six years old, and his dad died six years later. The rest of the family had to carry on with their lives. Daddy and his five brothers and sisters were trying to climb out of the Great Depression in time to prepare for the terrible events of World War II.

Many years later, I asked my Aunt Ollie about some of the family that Daddy always described as Scots-Irish. She told me my great-grandparents' names and the names of a few other ancestral relatives. But my husband and I moved often, so I lost that information. I remember that Daddy described his mother as a woman filled with laughter who came to the need of her neighbors at any time, day or night, as a practical nurse.

Daddy's father, Grandpa Mel Gaines, had auburn hair that I inherited with a tinge of red in my own. Grandpa

Mel was a painter, inside and outside, of homes and businesses. Following the Great Dayton Flood, he moved the family from Kentucky to Dayton, Ohio, in 1913. Everything that wasn't destroyed by the deep water had to be repainted.

My husband, Bill, was, and still is, a minister even in retirement. With our moving every four or five years, the small notes I had written were lost. With my profession as a counselor, we were often transferred to put out fires in local churches. I began to hate moving. I felt disconnected from family and community as the years went by.

As I said, my sister, Donna, first got the genealogy research bug. She was able to get the Gaines line back to our great-grandparents. But the Gaines line stopped with Great-great-grandpa Daniel George Gaines. We weren't even positive about that ancestor and completely uncertain about his wife, Katy, our great-great-grandmother.

Then Bill and I retired, moved out of the parsonage, and into our own home much closer to the huge genealogy library in Fort Wayne, Indiana. I dug through the files and reaffirmed one line that went back into antiquity through Great-grandma Jenny (Lee) Gaines. But we got stuck beyond a great-grandfather we lovingly called "1805 Daniel" and his wife, Great-grandma Jenny Lee. Who were 1805 Daniel Harry Gaines' parents?

When Ancestry offered the DNA test, I took it and sent it in. The results that came back were much like I expected.

First to catch my eye was the colorful pie-shaped circle chart that represented the countries from which my people came. The percentages are listed here.

| | |
|---|---|
| England & Northwestern Europe | 38% |
| Scotland | 35% |
| Wales | 12% |
| Ireland | 6% |
| Norway | 5% |
| Germanic Europe | 4% |

Since Ancestry DNA identifies only back to the fifth great-grandparents, Thomas Christopher Gowen, 1660-1726, was the last of my ancestors found through that wonderful scientific process. In total, DNA was able to identify ninety of my fifth great-grandparents. Thomas Christopher was the distant relative from which the Gaines family came. When they described Thomas Gowen as Black, European, and Cherokee, my mind couldn't wrap around that impossibility. If you add the above percentages, it's easy to see the total is 100 %. I had to find more to understand. I hungered for all I could find.

I was absolutely amazed. How could my family, who have mostly blondish/auburn or medium to light brown hair, fair skin, and mostly blue eyes, have a dark-skinned person as our ancestor? But something very exciting was also welling up inside me. After getting my DNA results, it felt like I

Fig. 2 Doris Gaines Rapp - Age 6

was a member of the whole human race, not just those in my own little bubble.

∙ ∙ ∙

If DNA results are as accurate as everyone says, I had to follow up with my own hours in front of my computer screen, I started to fill in the many blanks in my research. Using the internet to delve into medical issues, investigate legal problems, or even research genealogy is only as reliable as the sites you choose. Check your sources before making conclusions. In my ancestor seeking, I started searching through other paperwork besides the simple names and dates on the DNA report.

I did discover that race is a complicated identifier. More easily understood is skin color. Each person has between 20,000 and 25,000 genes. There are two genes that lead to skin depigmentation and therefore Europeans' white skin, SLC24A5 and SLC45A2. A third gene, HERC2/OCA2, causes blue eyes, and it contributes to light skin color and blonde hair.

We know that not all genes are passed down. Also, the amount of genetic material from one distant ancestor gets less and less as generations pass. I had to know more about my Gowen line.

∙ ∙ ∙

I found that Thomas Christopher's father, Mihill Gowen, was an indentured servant in colonial Jamestown. His mother, Prossa of the Ginkasquao, was also indentured. Then I discovered Mihill's father was John Goin/Gowen/Geaween. As you can see, John's last name had several spellings. His name at birth was João Geaween. João is Portuguese for John. For our purposes and because his son Mihill's surname was Gowen on my

DNA results, I will refer to Grandpa John only as John Gowen. .

John Gowen was born around 1605. According to Ric Murphy, an author, historian, Gowen genealogist, and descendent of John Gowen, said, "John was born in Kabasa, once the capital of the Kingdom of Ndongo, in the Angolan region of West Central Africa."

Kabasa was the royal seat of power at that time. The king of the Ngola dynasty lived there. A neighboring city, Ngoleme, is a little larger than Kettering, Ohio. Kabasa and Ngoleme were densely populated, with agricultural settlements surrounding them. The city people were skilled artisans and laborers such as blacksmiths and textile weavers. Many farmers had keen industrial knowledge, which was useful during non-planting and harvesting months.

Gowen landed at Point Comfort, where Hampton now sits, in the British Colonial Colony of Virginia in 1619 aboard the English privateer ship *White Lion*, making him one of the twenty to thirty original Africans in British North America. I'd like you to meet John Gowen, a Man of Significance.

## Chapter Two

### The Universal Family

A historian with the Jamestown-Yorktown Foundation was very helpful when we were in Virginia in April 2023. However, after she did a quick search, she was able to find just one John listed as a passenger on a 400-year-old list of the ship, the *James*. "John, a Negro. Passengers sent in the James for Virginia the last of July 1622". [1] The John she quickly uncovered had a different last name than our John, was three years older than John Gowen, and his contract was bought by a different planter. Also, other sources have revealed that two servants named John lived on the William Evans plantation. Also, later official colonial documents list John as a servant of William Evans. So, I will continue with John Gowen, Evans' servant.

John Gowen was identified on colonial muster rolls as an indentured servant. Many people have tried to find information about their enslaved ancestors, and some have reported that those who came to Virginia in 1619 could not have been indentured. They had to have been enslaved.

In 1619, there were no laws regarding enslaved people in the colonies. The Virginia Colony and the settlement at Jamestown were on an English charter. In the early 1600s, the English were familiar with the indentured system, in which people agreed to work for the holder of the indenture contract for a given number of years. The individual's length of servitude could have been a specific number of years, or the servant might work until they reached a given age. The colony had different rules for Native Americans. Their servitude had to end when the servant turned eighteen. The colonists needed the help of the indigenous people who lived nearby during the years of hunger. The servant's tribe would cooperate more if contracts were honored.

Another research source said that indentured servants who came after those in 1619 were mostly young men between the ages of fifteen and twenty-five. These men signed contracts in England to work in the colonies without wages until the cost of their passage to the New World was repaid. Up to seventy-five percent of all the individuals who made the transatlantic crossing in the seventeenth century were indentured servants.

In a dissertation, *The Free Negro in Virginia 1619-1865*, John Henderson Russell researched and explained the system of Indentured Servitude.[2] Russell submitted his work in 1913 to the Board of University Studies of Johns Hopkins University to complete the Degree of Doctor of Philosophy. Russell wrote, quoting John Rolf, a possible eyewitness to the arrival of the Angolans in Virginia:

"'About the last of August (1619) came in a Dutch man of Warre that sold us twenty [negroes].' In the very year of the arrival of this group of African immigrants, a system of labor known as indentured service received recognition in the laws of the colony.... Prior to 1619, every inhabitant of the colony was practically 'a servant manipulated in the interest of the company, held in servitude.'"

From the works of Captain John Smith, recorded in the Colonial Records of Virginia, Smith reported that the colony's first assembly provided that all contracts of servants should be recorded and enforced. That gave legislative recognition to servitude.[3]

The first servitude pertained to Native Americans who might come to a planter and request employment. The native might offer to provide food in the form of deer or fish from the river and streams. He could also beat corn and do other work as required.

The Assembly agreed to the native servant's work, providing no more than five or six were admitted to each plantation. In addition, a guard must be placed over them at night, given the many years of attacks by neighboring tribes. For their work, the plantation owner must provide separate housing for the natives and not interact with them socially. In addition, the Assembly encouraged each plantation to educate some native children and prepare them for confirmation in the Church of England.

The 1620 census, or muster, showed seventeen African women and fifteen African men in Jamestown. Although they were sold into servitude, many of the original Angolans fared better than the millions of Africans who followed. John Thorton, a Boston

University professor of African American Studies and History, reported:

"They had a better chance at a better future than almost anybody who followed them because they were the first." Thorton continued, "A lot of them ended up owning property, and they ended up owning slaves of their own."

"By intermingling with the English colonists, some had children who ended up passing for white and merging into early colonial society," Thorton said. [4]

Do not misunderstand. Those who signed on willingly did not include the first African captives who came to Virginia. Those who came with John Gowen in 1619 didn't indenture themselves to pay for their passage to the new world. John and the others didn't plan to leave their home. They were captured as spoils of war. And it certainly didn't include those who were captured in Africa and enslaved later in the colony's history, as the need for workers increased. That increased need brought more enslaved people to the colonies, and an increased number of the enslaved brought more slave laws, and an increase in slave laws brought more control for the planters, and more control often led to cruelty. As Lord Acton, a British historian of the late nineteenth and early twentieth centuries, said, "Absolute power corrupts absolutely." [5]

In early Angola, in 1617, the Portuguese governor, Luis Mendes de Vasconcelos, invited the Imbangala, a neighboring group, to act as a mercenary army to invade Angola. The army waged war over the next three years. The king of Angola was exiled.

In 1619, Grandpa John, and the other Angolans, were captured by the Portuguese and Imbangala. Portugal paid the Imbangala for their assistance. The Portuguese slave-ship, *São João Bautista,* left the port of São Paulo de Luanda, a Portuguese military outpost in West Africa, and sailed for Vera Cruz, New Spain (present-day Mexico). It carried 350 captured and enslaved Africans. The human cargo was to work in the tobacco fields of Mexico.

Between July and August 1619, two English ships, the *White Lion* and the *Treasurer*, both English privateer ships sailing out of the Netherlands, intercepted the Portuguese slave-ship *Bautista* off the coast of present-day Yucatán. The *White Lion* was operating under a Dutch letter of marque. A letter of marque and reprisal "was a government license in the Age of Sail that authorized a private person, known as a privateer or corsair, to attack and capture vessels of a nation at war with the issuer (the country that permitted the piracy)." [6] In other words, the ship's captain had papers that gave him the legal right to be a pirate. After stealing about sixty enslaved Africans from the Portuguese ship, *White Lion* and *Treasurer* sailed to the Virginia Colony to sell the enslaved there.

Various opinions exist about which ship John was on. It doesn't matter to me, as this book is about something other than claiming first-arrival status. It is just important to note that Grandpa John came to the New World against his will. Genealogy voices have claimed that the *White Lion* was Grandpa John's slave-ship to misery and the loss of all he was before.

When John and the other Angolan men, women, and children arrived in the Jamestown settlement, they were selected by tobacco growers who needed workers in their fields. The Black population had to grow as the need for enslaved people increased in the colonies. From then on, Blacks were kidnapped by other native Africans, not the Portuguese. The newly enslaved were sold to the English, who stacked them into the black hole of slave-ships like cordwood and brought them to the new, uncharted country.

To get to know my distant grandfather, I searched the history of his country of origin during the years he lived there. I read about the animals and topography he may have seen and the food he might have eaten. As I looked into his family, and later, when he had a wife and children, it confirmed that family love is universal. His work and experiences were also investigated. As a psychologist, I was naturally interested in the man as a person. Using research, I developed a possible Personality Sketch of my ancestor to make him real, and he touched my heart.

From all I read, John Gowen must have been quite intelligent, with an understanding of words, a command of the language, and an educated mind. From what I could find, he was an extraordinary man, a man of significance.

Is there a surprising ancestor in your family? Have you found someone through one of the DNA tests you had no idea sat on a branch of your family tree? Did you find the great-grandparent you've been looking for? Perhaps you discovered that Great-grandpa was the Gangland Strangler, yet you are the county District Attorney. Maybe your family has talked about "grumpy Great-grandpa" or "spooky old Great-Aunt Zelda." But do you really know that person? Or are you simply passing along family resentment, anger, envy, or hate? Is there someone who brought pain, humiliation, or financial ruin to your family? That ancestor is gone. Those negative feelings will only hurt you, not them. In this book, I have included writing prompts to help you get to know and understand your surprising family member like I have. By learning to forgive and accept them, you will be set free. For ancestors you knew nothing about, getting to know their home and circumstances will help you know and include them in your family. Making peace with the past is the best way to embrace the present and the future.

Before entering the Promised Land, God told Moses on Mount Sinai to create a year of Jubilee, a Sabbath Year, to occur every fifty years. The people were even to rest the land for a full year, as written in Leviticus 25: 1-4. And they were to do much more. God gave Moses a list of ways for those in need or enslaved to be helped. Then He added, "Even if someone is not redeemed in any of these ways, they and their children are to be released in the Year of Jubilee, for the Israelites belong to me as servants. They are my servants, whom I brought out of Egypt. I am the LORD your God." (Leviticus 25: 54-55 NIV)

Let this be our Year of Jubilee. Release those we hold captive through doubt or mistrust and turn our hate to love. After each chapter, think of three things to be thankful for because your ancestor was part of your family.

• • •

Years ago, I finally decided on the words to describe who I am. Far above my family of origin, "I am a child of the living God and disciple of Jesus, the Christ — a wife, mother, daughter, sister, and friend."

With John Gowen in my family lineage and those who came before and after him, the whole world seems like my family. I'm part of a greater community than my family, friends, and those in my little bubble. Who am I? What race am I? Like all of us, I am of the **Blessed** Race: *B*lessed, *L*oved, *E*ver *S*aved, *S*anctified, *E*xquisitely *D*esigned.

## Chapter Three

### Blessed

We know that our family lines have marched through time since creation. Isn't it amazing to think of those who have gone before us, their lives, mistakes, and accomplishments? I've heard some people say, "I'm not interested in ancestry. I live in the present, not the past."

Your genetic makeup includes a sprinkling of the genes from all those who went before you. You're creating a family tree, not a pedigree.

In response to an attendee's comment during a continuing education course I was teaching, a man said, "I don't know why so many of you are studying your genealogy. I'm Jewish. I know what tribe I come from."

Oh, to rest in the assurance of thousands of years of belonging. That is why people research their ancestral line. They want to know "the tribe they come from," the names and stories of their distant relatives.

Choose an ancestor you have heard about, found in a genealogical search, or were amazed to find in your DNA results. They, too, are blessed. This blessing is from the Lord God. It is not our blessing to take away. As you can see, I chose John Gowen, a man from Africa whom I did not know was in my family.

Sandra Baker Baron, an author-friend, wrote a wonderful book, *Bridging the Mississippi*. She tells an inspirational story of her time teaching in New Orleans. She and her husband, Denny, new college graduates and newly married, accepted teaching jobs in the South. While the students she taught and the adults who called her friend were not her ancestors, they became part of her family.

As you can see, to step outside of your bubble, you don't have to go back in history 400 or 500 years. Put your journey in reverse and go back to grandparents you didn't know, or people you knew but didn't understand. That could be the beginning of your life journey, outside you bubble.

I'll write a prayer of blessing here. Pray for your ancestor three times a day, like a blessing three times over, or taking cod liver oil as prescribed. It's your choice. Or, you can use the lines to create your own prayer to the One you know as Lord.

*Holy God, you are pure, creative love. I ask that you love and bless my family: those who went before and my family now, for all those in Heaven and on earth are yours. May anything I say, think or do not block their view of seeing you. I thank you for them, for you know the family I need, and those who need me. In the name of Jesus, your son, I pray. Amen*

Or, write your own prayer.

Doris Gaines Rapp, Ph.D.

_____
_____
_____
_____
_____
_____
_____
_____

Now write three things you're thankful for, because of your ancestor.

1._____
_____

2._____
_____

3._____
_____

# Africa

Fig. 3 Africa

## Chapter Four
### The New World

At first, my Ancestry's DNA report seemed impossible. How could a very English, Scottish, Welsh, and Irish person have a distant grandparent from Africa, born over four hundred years ago? I wanted to know more and more about these scientific outliers, John and his wife, Margaret Cornish. My seventh great-grandmother, Margaret, has nearly been lost in the distant past, but not John. I found only a few snippets about Margaret. But she lives on through her son, Mihill Gowen, his half-siblings, and all those who followed her. So, I started digging for information on John Gowen.

John Gowen was such a surprise to me. He may have had smooth dark skin and rich brown eyes like warm black opals that no doubt sparkled in the African sun. John could also have had very curly hair. His entire appearance would have differed from my fair, freckled skin that burns if I'm longer than fifteen minutes in the summer sun. My hair often refuses to curl even when I nearly fry it with the curling iron.

Fig. 4 Landing of the White Lion at Jamestown

John could also have had light brown skin due to central Africans taking partners with those much farther north. Remember, the Portuguese had tried to gain influence over Angola since the mid-1400s. Portugal planted a colony of one hundred families and four hundred soldiers in Angola in 1575. These Europeans also intermingled with the people of Angola, producing lighter-skinned Africans. John lived too far in the distant past, in the first American colonies, to know the answer. I think of him as very dark. To suggest an image of him, I chose the creative illustration by Valdir M, an Illustrator/Vector Artist, for the cover, so the reader can see John Gowen the way they think he may have appeared.

I was captivated by this relative embedded in my DNA. He was family, a long-lost beloved grandparent. He was Grandpa John. I had to know where he came from and what his life may have been like before he arrived in the New World.

I tried to read everything I could find. Many of the pieces were restatements of other sources. John Gowen and Margaret Cornish were on the *White Lion* or the *Treasurer*, English privateer ships.

Since John and Margret were in the group of first Africans to land in colonial America, much has been researched and written. Ten-year-old Margaret may have been on either ship. Researchers did not identify her ship. But John was on the *White Lion* and arrived in Jamestown Colony, British Colonial America, on August 20, 1619. That would have been a little more than a year before the *Mayflower* landed at Cape Cod on November 11, 1620. The Pilgrims began building their community in the spot where an Indigenous tribe, the Wampanoag people, had lived before most of the natives died of illness.

The discussion if John was actually on the *White Lion* is due to the fact the passenger list does not include his name. The list just counts the number of captured Angolans. Many Gowen family members believe John Gowen was on the ship that landed in 1619. It is not a matter of opinion. It is a matter of fact. He either was or he was not. However, official documents identify him by name as a resident of Jamestown in years to come.

You'll hear more about what John Gowen did after he arrived in the colonies. But first, I want to speculate about what his country of origin may have been like. My information is sketchy, but I'm a dreamer. As I read, I form mental pictures. I want to "see" the Angola, Africa, of 1619. Perhaps you are a descendant of John Gowen. I'm happy to share my imagination with you. I understand there are many of us.

The Gowen descendants are today described as Melungeons (m*uh*-**luhn**-j*uh*ns). In 2001, Tim Hashaw described the Melungeons as an ethnic group from the

Southeastern United States. Melungeons are descendants of Europeans, Native Americans, and sub-Saharan Africans. The latter came to America as indentured servants and later as enslaved people.[7] It is estimated that there are 200,000 Melungeons today. The Gowen family is the largest in this tri-racial population.

Hashaw added two important points.

1. To answer some confusion, Hashaw said the first Melungeons were in the Tidewater region of Virginia in 1619, not in the eighteenth century.

2. None of the Melungeon families traced back to a white plantation owner and a black enslaved woman. Freeborn blacks were the African ancestors of Melungeons for more than three hundred years.

Since the Gowen family is huge, reading or tracing all of John's descendants wouldn't be possible. That will have to be up to you. There are many research projects about this family. In Ric Murphy's YouTube presentation, "John Gowen's Descendants: Documenting America's Oldest African American Family," Mr. Murphy agreed. He said, "There are Gowen family members all across the country. We represent a multi-racial family of African American, Native American, and European Descent."[8]

John, although confronted with tragic circumstances, was a man of colonial Jamestown who made the very best of his life. I have no Bible records of births and deaths, or family stories to tell. I only have what I found through research. If I am wrong on any points, I do apologize. Grandpa John deserves better than that. Still, he is so interesting; I must tell you what I found. As you read about John Gowen, I hope you will be excited about finding your relatives, also lost in history.

Of my ninety fifth-great-grandparents, grandfathers, and grandmothers identified by DNA, eleven were from private Ancestry trees from which I could get no information. Seven great-grandparents were from England, one was from Scotland, three were from Ireland, and seven were from Germany. Of those ninety great-grandparents, fifty-four were of European descent but were born in various British American colonies. What nationality am I? One could look at the numbering of my most distant ancestors and say, "She's a subject of the King of England. She's English, Scotch, and Irish." Since the original men who established the English colony of Jamestown were part of the Virginia Company, they, too, were from the British Isles. However, a larger slice of the genealogical pie does not make me British. Nor am I German, Angolan, or Cherokee. I am Blessed. I am an American, and my colonial ancestors were colonial Americans. Still, I was absolutely fascinated with Grandpa John Gowen.

## Chapter Five
### Who Are Your People?

Who are your people? You must have an ancestor you know little or nothing about. Perhaps you or your family members have never been caught by the fascination of genealogy. You may have to grow old enough to wear purple to become curious about your ancestors. The reality may be that you had no time to spend hours in the library when you were younger. Now, with the internet and various sites offering DNA testing, you don't have to leave home to find your people.

• • •

My husband, Bill, and I had three birth children, adopted another boy when he was nearly ten, and later, adopted two baby girls. Our youngest daughter isn't even thirty-five now, yet the genealogy bug bit her. She knows her family and has heard stories about them for many years.

Now she wants information on her bloodline to complete her sense of who she is. Her family is my husband and I, two brothers, and three sisters. But who are her DNA ancestors?

I think about Grandpa John and the loss of his bloodline. His search would be like adopted children, who may wonder if every familiar looking older man in the mall just might be their birth father.

I'm curious if John questioned any of the captives who came to the colony on slave-ships in later years, asking if they might be related to him. Had they known his parents? Were his parents well? Did his father still create the most artful wooden spoons? Did his mother continue to grill the fish his father brought up on the end of his fishing line? Were the white tilapia filets grilled over an open flame in the yard making the whole world smell rich, crisp, and wonderful? Eaten with ripe plantain and sweet potato, John probably remembered how it filled his stomach. If John knew his family was safe, happy, and well, it would make him feel safe and complete.

I certainly saw that with our adopted children. To help them be grounded, by the time our youngest daughters were toddlers, they had met and spent a little time with their birth father. Their birth mother lived a thousand miles away.

One summer, our family went to King's Island for a day of fun. I saw a young boy who looked like our adopted son, with blond curly hair and a broad smile. I encouraged him to approach the boy. Our son couldn't gather the courage to talk to the young teenager who may have been his older brother, but he wanted to. We all look for family when they are lost.

Now, years later, both of our adopted daughters are excited about finding their people. Perhaps one of their ancestors will surprise or fascinate them. You, the readers, can follow the research sections I have included in the book, using the prompts to lead you to other questions, and down other research paths.

Get to know a distant relative. You might also want to use the worksheets to begin to understand a relative you don't like or couldn't understand why he or she was as they were. Do you harbor negative feelings about them?

Fear

Hate

Mistrust

Inferiority

Superiority

Anger

In reality, that distant relative is part of you. You have their genes inside you to a large or small extent. Your hate and fear can eat away at you, not at your ancestor. Free yourself from that darkness by forgiving, loving, and wrapping family arms around them. Rejoice and embrace your unknown relative. You cannot love yourself and hate others. Love and hate are opposites.

Are you indifferent to distant relatives? Are you one of those, "I live in the present," people? You could miss knowing someone as interesting as John Gowen.

Now that we have experienced an amazing connection to all of God's people because we are Blessed, we can begin to get to know others around us by first learning about one we never knew existed. In today's world, we hardly know our neighbors. For a nice dinner at a restaurant, we dress in casual-pressed clothes and dressy shoes, then stick a cell phone in front of our faces.

My challenge is for you to find one of your ancestors and get to know them through research. We cannot show understanding, sympathy, or acceptance of others if we know nothing about them as a group or an individual. The point is to learn about a great-grandparent, or farther back, whom you didn't know before. They may be from a different country, race, or ethnicity, have talents you never dreamed of having, or have a physical limitation or a disability that has defined their life. You might think of another category for someone in your genealogy or family stories that surprised you.

As you find information, accept them as family, part of your genetic line. Love them like they are your beloved grandparent with whom you used to go to the circus or listen to stories as they read. Now begin by using these prompts to discover more about a distant relative. I have left space for you to add information unique to your ancestor. If you prefer, purchase a notebook to complete the prompts that help you get to know your distant relative.

Name of ancestor:

_____

Relationship to you:

_____

Date of Birth:

_____

Date of Death:

___

Where were they born?

___

Where did they die?

___

What was their occupation?

___

Father's name:

___

Father's job and unique factors about them:

___
___

Mother's name:

___

Mother's job and unique factors about them:

___
___

Other information you found

___
___
___

Doris Gaines Rapp, Ph.D.

_____
_____
_____
_____
_____

 *Holy God, you are pure, creative love. I ask that you love and bless my family: those who went before and my family now, for all those in Heaven and on earth are yours. May anything I say, think or do not block their view of seeing you. I thank you for them, for you know the family I need, and those who need me. In the name of Jesus, your son, I pray. Amen*

Or, write one of your own.

_____
_____
_____
_____
_____
_____
_____

A Man of Significance

Now write three things you're thankful for, because of the ancestor you are researching.

1._____

_____

2._____

_____

3._____

_____

## Chapter Six
### The Land of Ndongo/Angola

John Gowen's home of Angola, in southwestern Africa, is the historic home of the Mbundu people. The main part of the original kingdom was in the highlands east of Luanda, Angola, between the Cuanza and Lucala rivers. The kingdom's land space stretched west to the Atlantic coast and south of the Cuanza when John Gowen lived there. The rolling, ever consistent waves of the incoming tide to the west and the majestic mountains were familiar sites in John's world.

Grandpa John would have called that entire mass of land, home. I wonder what part of that varied landscape young John would have run through chasing his dog, the faithful animal's ears erect, with long legs and a short coat. I also think about how far John Gowen would have traveled on foot. Did the family have a horse or other animal on which he could ride?

We believe John's family lived in Kabasa, so perhaps he was close enough to walk to markets. Within Kabasa, he would have had access to the news of the day. We know from Bible passages that even ancient people walked in groups or caravans to larger cities to register for the census or visit a temple for worship.

*Fig. 5 Angola (Ndongo), Africa*

Old movies often depicted the people of Africa as uneducated, savage, isolated people in primitive huts far from civilization and information about their country. That may not have been true of John Gowen. Granted,

John lived in Angola four hundred years ago. Most people lived in villages away from the bustle of cities. While John's home and living conditions are unknown to me, I believe he had access to some education in Kabasa. I am basing my guess on John's abilities and responsibilities much later in life in British Colonial America. And, as I said, military attacks would have come to the more populated areas. John and the other captives were spoils of war. They could have been gathered up from the streets and lanes of Kabasa.

Angola's landscape was beautiful, with primitive vegetation growing everywhere.

*Fig. 6 Slaves in Africa*

When a mercenary army, hired by the Governor to attack Angola, kidnapped John and the other men, women, and children, they led the captives west to the ocean. John may have been so traumatized that he might have been oblivious to his surroundings. He and the other captives were marched to the port on the ocean to embark on a ghastly slave-ship. They too may have been in shock over their plight and saw nothing. They would cross the deep and choppy waters of the fierce Atlantic from the coast.

Angola's many land areas included the semidesert Atlantic littoral (lit-er-*uhl*) or seacoast. There, the black-browed albatross sailed across the open salt sky on their six-foot wingspan.

That area borders Namibia's "Skeleton Coast," the land that is now the sparsely populated rainforest interior. They call it the Skeleton Coast because of the whale bones found there, along with hundreds of wrecked and broken ships scattered on the beach.

In John's time, the rainforest would have been lush, with a dense stand of trees that probably smelled lush. The silence of the swaying branches would make other sounds around them clear and sharp. The thick stand of trees in the rainforest 400 years ago was mainly in the northern part of the Cabinda exclave, the western edge of the Malanje (m*uh*-lan-j*uh*) highlands, the northwestern corner of the Bié Plateau, and along some rivers in the northeast.

Today the rainforest has been thinned drastically. Since half of neighboring Namibia's people are rural, they have cut down the trees to build homes and other shelters, chop firewood, and secure food and medicines. Based on the items archeologists found in the area, they made kitchen utensils and other household items from that wood for hundreds of years. Planting new trees, and forest management, were apparently not practiced by the Angolans at that time in history.

Angola also enjoys the rugged highlands (or mountainous areas) in the country's south. Mount Moca, at 2,600 meters (8,530 feet), is located in the Huambo Province in the western part of the country and is the highest mountain in Angola. While it is dwarfed by Mount Kilimanjaro in Tanzania, Africa, at 5,895 meters (19,340 feet), Angola is proud of the mountain. It draws people who enjoy its peak. Mount Moca was named one of Angola's seven wonders in 2014.

I'm curious if Grandpa John ever tried to climb any of the mountains or how far the peaks were from his home. I know my husband and son, Jim, at age fourteen, would have climbed as high as they could. See in your mind the struggle and strength it would take to reach the top of the mountain. Once you are at the top, turn around and view the beautiful green foliage stretched out in front of you, against the blue, unpolluted sparkling sky, from high above the tops of the majestic trees.

The Cabinda exclave, separated from the rest of the country, was in the north. An exclave is a portion of the country separated from the main part, like Alaska is detached from the lower forty-eight. Densely settled towns and cities are now on the northern coast of Angola and north-central river valleys.

How far would the villagers and our John Gowen have hiked into that vast playground of tall trees, and how high would he have climbed? As I found through research, regardless of how far they would have hiked, the rainforest would have been gradually pushed farther back into remaining trees as the people harvested the timber.

## Chapter Seven
### The Land Your Early Family Called Home

I know you have been reading about your family's country of origin. Write on the lines below something new you learned about that country of long ago. Are there unique formations? With a country as large as the United States, you could list the oceans, lakes, and mountains. There are caverns, caves, ancient indigenous dwellings, and burial sites. If your country is also large list what interests you the most, or something you previously knew nothing about. The Jamestown-Yorktown Foundation built a true-to-size replica of the historic fort near the original site of Jamestown, Virginia, in 1619. My husband and I visited there in April 2023.

My fifth great-grandmother was Cherokee, and by chance, my husband and I visited the capital of the Eastern Band of the Cherokee Nation a few years ago. It's one and a half hours from Hendersonville, in Cherokee, North Carolina. The Easter Band is only one of three Cherokee tribes recognized in the United States.

Sometimes mistaken as a "Cherokee Indian Reservation," it is also known as Qualla Boundary and was purchased by the tribe in the 1870s.

Where had your ancestor lived that you could visit? If you can't go there in person, are there documentaries or YouTube videos you could enjoy? Search the library for books with illustrations of your family's country of origin. Imagine yourself there, then write some descriptions here.

_____

_____

_____

_____

_____

_____

_____

_____

_____

_____

_____

_____

A Man of Significance

Attach pictures you may find here.

Doris Gaines Rapp, Ph.D.

*Holy God, you are pure, creative love. I ask that you love and bless my family: those who went before and my family now, for all those in Heaven and on earth are yours. May anything I say, think or do not block their view of seeing you. I thank you for them, for you know the family I need, and those who need me. In the name of Jesus, your son, I pray. Amen*
Or, write one of your own.

_____

_____

_____

_____

_____

_____

_____

Now write three things you're thankful for, because of your ancestor.
1._____

_____

2._____

_____

3._____

_____

# Chapter Eight
## John Gowen's Homeland

How I wish I could close my eyes and see the tall grass on the hills John Gowen would have run through as a boy in Angola, the green leafing trees he would have climbed, just as I did as a child.

My friend Nancy lived across the street from my childhood home. Her backyard had the best apple tree. Its lowest branch stretched out like the riding saddle on a great stallion. I'd ride my imaginary sorrel beauty through my fanciful play and the dreamy fields of home. I wonder if Grandpa John did the same.

I also remember laying on a blanket in the backyard on a warm summer afternoon, watching the clouds float by. I could see animals, people, and all kinds of imaginary shapes in the white, fluffy, cotton-shaped cumulus clouds overhead. My friends and I would point out those hidden images that others didn't look up to see or couldn't find if they searched the sky. John Gowen didn't need his imagination to see interesting sites. They were all around him.

• • •

I like to imagine Grandpa John sitting on the edge of a forest in the early morning hours, watching a red-tailed monkey. The red color of the two-toned tail would have been visible on the underside, from dark grey at the base to increasing red at the tip of the tail. John may have stopped to watch the white-nosed monkey swing through the canopy of the trees. John could have laughed as the large monkey's white, elastic cheeks stretched out from his dark face, bulging with bananas and mangos it had stored there. Since red-tailed monkeys liked to stay in the trees rather than occasionally foraging on all four legs on the ground, they were extremely active, swinging very fast from branch to branch. Can't you see John's wide smile as the monkeys communicate physically, vocally, and visually? The monkeys sounded like birds, chirping a message to other primates in their large social group. It might have been easy for John to determine the dominant monkey from the submissive ones as the stronger male took the lead, like in their search for food. Red-tailed monkeys are omnivorous, so their search for fruit dominates their day. Then, if they couldn't find any fruit, they sometimes ate leaves, flowers, or even insects.

Fig. 7 Red-tailed monkey

Two of the 308 plants or fruits the red-tailed monkey may have eaten were papayas and tomatoes. Yes, the wonderful red fruit some families call a vegetable is the same tomato that grows in Angola. John may have pulled

## A Man of Significance

one off the vine, rubbed it on his breeches, and bit into the smooth skin as he passed the garden. Other plants and flowers that may attract the monkey could be the beautiful evergreen flowering plants.

Fig. 8 Aardvark

The aardvark, sometimes called the antbear, might also entertain young John. It's a stocky animal whose name means "earth pig" because of its piglike face and habit of burrowing. Animals filled John's world. He may have led an exciting life among the crocodiles in the shallow area at the water's edge. John would have avoided the cape buffalo with its unpredictable behavior. An undomesticated buffalo was not a pet. Its strange horns made it very distinctive. The horns were fused at the base, forming a continuous boney brace across the top of its head just above the forehead.

Fig. 9 Cape Buffalo

John lived in a wonderland of animals. I don't know how many four-footed strays came into the small villages and larger towns. I would imagine there were fence boundaries, like a fort against intruders. I can only guess that there were ways to keep the wild animals out, or very few Angolans would have survived. Did the adder get close? Were African lions, black rhinos, or hippos seen anyplace near the village? Whether John saw any of the exotic animals or if the beasts kept their distance from people, John would have been wise enough to give them the space they demanded.

I'm sure if you or I saw those animals in a zoo, it would produce an admiration much different than coming upon them in the wild. Fenced areas are safer than sharing a lonely path with a dangerous animal away from the safely enclosed village.

The giant sable antelope was beautiful, with long curved horns. Even though magnificent, if it crossed John's path, he gave the antelope the right-of-way. Today, very few huge sable antelopes remain.

Fig. 10 Giant Sable Antelope

I wondered if Angola had fireflies for young John to watch and chase in the cooler temperatures of the evening. Of course, the many mosquitos may have dampened the joy of some of those nights. But that's no different than it is here in the United States. What a wonderful world of animals and birds he grew up in.

Some of the birds were vastly different from the ones we have here. Angola was home to the non-flying, funny-running ostriches, and the albatross some have written poems about. I was curious about everything in the country John called home.

• • •

My Ohio home was a safe and carefree place to grow up. As a ten-year-old, I'd take the city bus downtown to see a movie or shop. Sometimes, I bought another piece of doll furniture at my favorite dime store.

When I was six or seven, the transit would carry me to the skating rink a few miles away for an afternoon of

## A Man of Significance

fun with friends and an exercise in independence. I never knew until I was an adult that my father followed the bus in his car each time to ensure I got off at the right stop.

A few years later, on Saturday mornings, I'd ride the bus to the National Cash Register Company, the NCR, where they offered free movies to any Dayton child who could get there. The NCR auditorium held over 2000 people. As the moviegoers left the building, young ushers passed out free candy bars to every girl and boy who came to see Roy Rogers and the Riders of the Purple Sage catch the wrestlers and have fun. I wondered where John went for entertainment and what the activity would have been.

The animals in my world were my dog, Spotty, a mixed-breed cocker spaniel, and an occasional rabbit or squirrel that ran through the yard. Do you see why I found Grandpa John so intriguing?

• • •

I also wondered what kind of food John would have eaten. What did his mother cook? My reading discovered, besides the familiar tomato, there were other foods similar to what we dine on today. The most common plant in Angola included the cowpea, an annual grain legume (like beans and peas). They also grew peppers and sweet basil and used them in cooking. What dishes would his mother have prepared with the green pepper? Perhaps she stuffed them with chicken, pork, or a mix of other vegetables.

Some non-eatable plants were the garden croton, a showy indoor or outdoor plant. The snake plant, although poisonous, is very eye-catching. The poisonous dieffenbachia, with its beautiful foliage, is lovely and grows in other countries as well. The Zanzibar gem is a

Doris Gaines Rapp, Ph.D.

flowering indoor green plant. But the heart of Jesus plant is deceiving. It's a poisonous leafy plant with heart-shaped leaves. One thinks of love when admiring it, not poison. The Madagascar periwinkle and Chinese hibiscus are other plants that grow in Angola.

    I knew very little about Africa before I became driven to know and understand all I could about my people. I knew even less about Angola. Yet, I wanted to know something about the home from which John came. John's home of origin helped mold him into who he became. Even his status in that society, and that of our family, can have a lasting effect. For some, a lower social status forever traps the individual in that class. Others rise above their circumstances and make a better life for themselves and their family. I will not pretend to have made an extensive study of Africa. What little I could find on the Internet; I am describing here.

    As we review a little history of the country in John's time, I encourage you not to skip this section of the book because the names are foreign or hard to pronounce. Show respect for the differences between Angola and your home. Names are our first recognition of personal identity.

• • •

    Before graduate school, I was an educator. In my first year out of undergraduate school, I taught a second-grade class in a small rural school in the Mesilla Valley of New Mexico. I reviewed the class list of my thirty-two second graders before school started and saw names I couldn't pronounce. That evening, I dug my tape recorder out of the closet and took it to school the next day.

# A Man of Significance

"We're going to record a 'man on the street' interview," I explained to the class. "Like on television, I'll ask your name and what you did this summer. We can then take turns listening to the sound of our voice on the recording."

My real motive with the tape recorder was learning to pronounce each name before I insulted the children with a chopped-up version of the word that so personally identified them. Laughter filled the classroom each time I told my class that my family and I had visited Juárez, Mexico, the previous Saturday. I had botched the pronunciation of Juárez as only a Midwesterner could.

Vocal music was my college minor, so, driving back and forth from school to home, I would practice the beautiful rhythm in each connecting syllable of all thirty-two names, like Severiano and Primitivo. First, I hung the vowels on the beats, then the consonants. Names are very important. With our study of the history of Grandpa John's homeland, pronunciation without offense is important.

Discovering names, food, and life in Africa were all new learning experiences for me. And I have only touched the outer rim of the vast knowledge I'd like to learn. I hope you find your study of a chosen ancestor as fascinating. They came to America at some point, most for a better life. I wondered what their social position and opportunities were in the country they called home.

Doris Gaines Rapp, Ph.D.

## Chapter Nine
### Your Search for Your Ancestor's Homeland

To know someone, we must know what has helped to inform their lives. The home where they grew up is a major part of what made them who they are. You have identified your ancestor; now get acquainted with their homeland by filling these spaces.

Plants:
_____
_____
_____
_____

Flowers:
_____
_____

A Man of Significance

Animals:

Birds:

Landscape of home:

How might your ancestor have felt about their home?

Doris Gaines Rapp, Ph.D.

_____

_____

What might your ancestor have done for fun?

_____

_____

_____

_____

_____

Find some pictures and either add them here or sketch some elements you find interesting.

*Holy God, you are pure, creative love. I ask that you love and bless my family: those who went before, and my family now, for all those in Heaven and on earth are yours. May anything I say, think, or do, not block their view of seeing you. I thank you for them, for you know the family I need, and those who need me. In the name of Jesus, your son, I pray. Amen*
Or, write your own.

_____
_____
_____
_____
_____
_____
_____

Now write three things you're thankful for, because of your ancestor.

1._____
_____

2._____
_____

3._____
_____

# Chapter Ten
## Social Structure

An investigation into the social structure of John Gowen's native home was very enlightening. My uneducated perception of everyday life in Africa saw people living happily in family units, 400 to 500 years ago, with no concerns. But then, I always see life from a very positive point of view. My research revealed a more sophisticated social system than I imagined. After reading, I wondered if John Gowen was free while still living in Angola. That question seemed odd. If you were like me, I assumed all Africans were free in their home country.

From britannica.com, I read that sixteenth-century records list the Kimbundu-speaking area as the land of Mbundu. Angola divided the region into 736 small political units ruled by sobas, which were leaders who controlled the small territories and the lives of those who lived there. Those territories, called munindo, were clusters or groupings of villages that surrounded a small

## A Man of Significance

town central to all. By the sixteenth century, the rulers of Angola united these larger kingdoms. Kabasa, located on the highlands near modern-day N'dalatando, was the capital.

Those are a lot of words that most of us have never heard before but take your time. Have fun with your pronunciation of these elements of history. You and I may not be correct in our attempt to speak the names, but the places become more real when we hear them spoken. At least try.

The king and the leaders of the provinces ruled with the support of a council of powerful nobles called the macota. Cities in America have their system of mayor and city council. However, officials in the United States are elected.

The administration's head in the land of Mbundu was a judicial figure called the tendala, and the ngolambole, a military leader. The "government" sounds organized and well-developed to meet the needs of most.

They had a strict system for identifying population groups in those days, 500 years ago. The basic principle of the social structure was "ana murinda," or children of murinda, free commoners. They also had two other groups, both servile, the ijiko — the unfree commoners, or serfs forever tied to the land, and the abika (singular - mubika), the salable slaves. [9]

A very loose comparison with farm communities in the south of the United States in the eighteenth century would help. Some landowners passed family farms down through generations. Tenant farmers rented land they could farm from another landowner. The tenant farmer received two-thirds to three-quarters of the harvest minus living expenses. Another group, sharecroppers, didn't own the house or the land. They received only half of the crop. From the crop sale, the landowner deducted rent and any credit, plus interest, for supplies provided for the family's subsistence. Last, the enslaved people owned nothing and received very little for their work. Once a month, the plantation owner passed out a few pieces of clothing. And once a week, a ration of food was distributed for the enslaved and their family.

People have enslaved others even back in antiquity. One of the first records of enslaved people was in the Mesopotamian and Sumerian civilizations, located in what is now the Iran/Iraq regions, as far back as 6000-2000 BC. Unsurprisingly isolated areas like the countries in fifteenth century Africa would still enslave people. However, the Angolans Portugal seized and sent to the New World in 1619 were from each social groups: commoners, serfs, and the enslaved. As stated, the abika were salable enslaved people, and the Angolans did sell them as captives to the Portuguese. But the abika were kidnapped along with the ijiko and the commoners.

Portugal tried to take over Angola for over a century. Portugal's interest was all about the slave trade.

## Chapter Eleven
### Slave History in Your Ancestor's Country-of-Origin

What was the history of enslaving people in the country where your people come from? From what "class" did your distant relative come? What were their advantages and disadvantages. Research the country from which your people came in general and discover any interesting facts you can find about their class system and enslaved people.

_____
_____
_____
_____
_____
_____
_____
_____

Doris Gaines Rapp, Ph.D.

_____

_____

*Holy God, you are pure, creative love. I ask that you love and bless my family: those who went before and my family now, for all those in Heaven and on earth are yours. May anything I say, think, or do, not block their view of seeing you. I thank you for them, for you know the family I need and those who need me. In the name of Jesus, your son, I pray. Amen*
Or, write your own.

_____

_____

_____

_____

_____

_____

_____

Now write three things you're thankful for, because of your ancestor.
1._____

_____

2._____

_____

3._____

_____

## Chapter Twelve
### Portugal's Attempts at Colonization

To understand someone, we need to know how, as well as where, they grew up. Our experiences and how those events shaped our lives as citizens of the United States would be vastly different from those born into a very repressed country where individual freedom was not valued or non-existent.

Angola's struggle with Portugal had been part of the people's lives for many generations. There were multiple invasions, with mighty ships of war approaching the shore time and again. John may have frequently watched the ships with their large, broad sails on the water and wondered where their cannon balls would land.

The need for captives to supply the demand of the slave trade was constant. A new shipload of workers for the tobacco fields of Mexico sailed from Luanda frequently. Portugal bought their captured innocent people in Angola. The country experienced much unrest from Portugal during the many years that Portugal tried to colonize Angola.

It was complicated. Portugal was a colonizer, plus a possible ally to protect Angola from the many attacks by Kongo. With the Portuguese influence on the country, Kongo was soon renamed Congo. Warrior aggression from that neighboring country put Angola on constant guard. The attackers regularly kidnapped the Angolans and sold them as enslaved people in South America.

John Gowen's great-grandparents may even have been aware of missing family members or the children of friends and other people who were kidnapped and shipped off during the night. In 1518, one hundred years before the Portuguese seized John as a war trophy, the Kingdom of Angola attempted to enlist the help of Portugal as they struggled for freedom from Congo. Hoping to get on the good side of the Catholic European country, Angola sent an embassy to Portugal asking for missionaries. They also wanted to be recognized as independent from Congo. If Portugal was going to interfere in the lives of the Angolan people, then perhaps that European country could sever the vassal relationship Angola had with Congo.

The group who went to Portugal knew it was very important to Portugal that the missionaries baptize the enslaved people before they left Africa. If Angola offered baptism before being forced to comply, it might ensure their separation from Congo.

It is hard to believe that people in the small villages would have known the political and military trouble between their homeland and Portugal. Obviously, there were no Amber alerts on newscasts or in newspapers. Yet, we know from Bible records that travelers passed the news to people along the trade routes. Angolan villagers would have been aware of missing children and young adults from their communities, lost to slave traders. The lack of a cell phone does not equal a lack of knowledge.

We have already reviewed society's three classes in Angola, the commoners, or free people, the serfs, and the enslaved people that they sold. However, the 1518 connection with the emissary from Angola to Portugal was unsuccessful.

• • •

Less than fifty years later, in 1556, Angola sent another group to Portugal asking for military assistance. Those from Angola offered baptism again.

Four years later, in 1560, another mission group from Portugal arrived at the mouth of the Cuanza River under the leadership of the grandson of the European explorer Bartolomeu Dias, Paulo Dias de Novais. That group included the Jesuit priest Francisco de Gouveia. Dias de Novais tried to fulfill the task of putting Angola more tightly under the thumb of Portugal. However, that mission failed as the previous one had, and Dias de Novais sailed home in 1564, leaving the priest, Gouveia, behind in Angola.

That wasn't the end of Portugal's desire to subjugate Angola. The Angolan people had their safety and security threatened again. During a third mission in 1571, the King of Portugal, Sebastian I, ordered Dias de Novais to subjugate the Kingdom of Angola, govern the region, bring in settlers, and build forts. Dias de Novais arrived in Luanda by arrangement with Congo's King Alvaro I in compensation for Portugal's assistance against the Jago, or invading bands of African warriors east and south of the kingdom of Congo. Portugal tried to repay Congo for their help in the struggle against the Jago. As a result, Quilongo, the King of Angola, renewed his connection with Portugal in 1578. However, Portugal could not conquer any territory alone, so Dias de Novais made alliances with Congo and Angola serving as a mercenary army.[10]

The first Portuguese-Angolan War was in 1579. As a result, in 1599, Portugal and Angola established a formalized border between Congo and Angola, finally identifying the unique and separate countries.

• • •

There were constant wars and rumors of war. In the early 1600s, Portugal and Angola had a very slippery peace. But the Portuguese continued to expand their territory into west central Africa.

Notice this next date carefully. Remember that John Gowen came to the colonies in 1619. It was in 1617 when Luis Mendes de Vasconcelos, the governor of Angola, first rejected the plan to use the neighboring Imbangala troops against Angola. Then he changed his mind, committed to the alliance, and aggressively moved against Angola. With Imbangala warriors' help, the governor invaded Angola, sacked the capital, and forced King Ngola Mbandi to take refuge on the island of Kindonga in the Kwanza River.[11]

During the aggression, they took thousands of Angolan people prisoner. However, Mendes de Vasconcelos was unsuccessful in creating a puppet government under the rule of Portugal.[12] Negotiations between Portugal and Angola continued for the next few years.

# A Man of Significance

The Angolan subjects kidnapped during the invasion were not seized for the slave trade, although their fate was the same. The capture of those Angolan people was part of war practices. John Gowen and Margret Cornish were probably two who were captured as a winner-take-all award practice and sent off to Mexico.

• • •

For those of you who have done a much broader study of Angola than I, you will be familiar with the warrior queen, Nzinga. The queen's name is written Nzinga and Njinga. I will use Nzinga. Any history of Angola must include Nzinga Mbandi due to her help in the country's crises. Nzinga was the sister of Governor Mendes de Vasconcelos' successor, Joao Correia de Sousa. Nzinga negotiated a peace treaty with Portugal. In the treaty, Portugal agreed to withdraw its advance fort, return many captive ijiko (serfs) to Angola, and force the Imbangala bands, who continued to attack Angola, to leave. In return, Nzinga's brother, Ngola Mbandi, could leave the island to where he was exiled and return to the capital. Mbandi agreed that Angola would become a Portuguese vassal and pay 100 slaves per year in tribute. [13] It appears that Nzinga had to pay in slaves to succeed in the first step of a more permanent peace for Angola.

Notice that the captured people that the Portuguese returned were serfs, not the enslaved, or commoners. Capturing serfs was a far different practice than supplying people for the slave trade.

After John had been in the colony for five years, sometime after 1624, upon her brother's death, Nzinga Mbandi (1581-1663) became the Queen of Ndongo (Angola) and Matamba. Later she also became a fearless warrior queen, skilled negotiator, and outstanding military general. She fought against the Portuguese as they expanded their slave trade in Central Africa.

By that time in Angola's history, Grandpa John may have heard about the war in Angola from the newly enslaved as they arrived. But, as you can see, John's entire childhood was spent under the threat of war, invasions from neighboring countries, and a fear of slave marauders. His belief in a safe world would have differed from yours or mine. John would have had to learn to depend on his own ingenuity and intelligence rather than his community's ability to protect him.

I have given you this history of Angola so that you and I may understand more about John Gowen because of who he became and how he later served the people of British Colonial America.

## Chapter Thirteen
### Religion of Angola

Religion, or my relationship with Jesus, is the major part of my life. I had to know where John drew his strength and what filled his heart.

The Mbundu had not recorded their language into written form until the Jesuit missionaries carefully penned it. The Jesuits arrived with the Portuguese colonizers in 1575, hoping to convert West Central Africans to Christianity. As with most societies, the Mbundu people already had their own beliefs. At the center of their religion was their belief that the souls of their dead ancestors (zumbi) continued to influence the living world after they had departed. John, his family, and the people around them believed they could communicate with their dead relatives at the ancestor's grave. That doesn't cancel the introduction of Roman Catholicism the Portuguese brought to Angola. The missionaries were careful not to insult the native religion of the people.

Another influence on the people was their deities, called ilundu. The ancient, traditional religion in West Central Africa did recognize a creator or high god. But with those beliefs, the people did not see their god as active in the world. In Congo, they called the creator Nzambi a Mpungu. However, there were supernatural beings who were active in their lives. They were ancestral spirits, local deities, and lesser spirits that maliciously bothered the living. The lesser spirits sound like mischievous beings we've all heard about in other cultures.

Holy sites, or shrines, were built for the ilundu so the people had a place to worship them. I wondered what the shrines looked like. Were they buildings or grottoes made of stone?

The leaders did not centralize their religion, or place the control and interpretation under the clergy as one might think of a denomination today. There was no connectional system with the church communities.

The Jesuits introduced Christianity into West Central Africa with respect for the people's ancestral beliefs. A review of the growing Christian presence in that part of Africa indicated it began during the reign of Afonso Mvemba Nzinga (1504–1542). In 1491, after the Portuguese explorer Diogo Cão arrived in Congo and Angola, Nzinga Nkuwu, also known as João I, was king He became the first baptized manikongo, or king of Congo. Congo was under a growing Portuguese influence for a long time, beginning in the late fifteenth and early sixteenth centuries. Remember, Angola was a vassal state to Congo. Mwene Kongo Nzinga Nkuwu's baptism resulted in acquiring and integrating Christianity rituals and symbols into their religion. West Central Africa was being Christianized in the late 1400s and educated by the Jesuits with the creation of literature in their language such as religious forms, pamphlets, and literature. [14]

Since armies waged war against the largest cities, the first Angolans and John Gowen's lives in Kabasa made them likely targets for capture, but also beneficiaries of the church's education.

As Ric Murphy said, "They were Catholic, and many spoke multiple languages." He continued speaking about John Gowen and his descendants. "They came from a royal city and were quite informed and educated, and several of them, based upon what they did in the latter part of their years, clearly were leaders in the community in one form or the other," Murphy said. "Many of them became landowners, which is quite different from the false narrative of what an enslaved person was." [15]

In today's religious communities, like the Southern Baptists, all have similar beliefs, as do Roman Catholics, and many Protestant denominations. In West Central Africa, each individual or community had their own understanding and beliefs about their religion, although certain elements of the religion were present in all. Those who were Catholic were more similar in their beliefs.

One component in general society was uniform to all people, the Military. Military training would have been a part of everyone's lives, given their many years of unrest with Portugal and the frequent battles with other African nations.

In modern-day Angola, the population is Christian. Two-fifths are Roman Catholic, two-fifths are Protestant, and about one-tenth follow the traditional beliefs of past generations or other religions. Britannica [16] identified the religious makeup of Angola as rooted in the country's history. Of course, that would be true. As people of a specific faith move into an area, they may influence their neighbors with new teaching.

In 1619 Angola, music and dance were two vital parts of their religion and everyday lives. The music of West Central Africans was sophisticated, using complex rhythms, horns, stringed instruments, and marimbas. Those who played the drums were highly skilled.

I close my eyes and wonder if John played an instrument. He could have made a drum from a beautiful tree burl; hollowed it; then polished it, and stretched an animal skin across the top. Or, he may have drilled seven holes in a length of bamboo, creating a mellow sounding flute. Would he have gathered plants or berries to create paint with which to decorate his instrument with flowers or fun animals?

Did he dance with grace and rhythm? Most of us would agree that beautiful, spirit-filled music continues to be a major part of the Christian church.

Music has always filled my life. Besides years of vocal lessons, I also always wanted to dance. But I couldn't even cross and backcross the steps in a country line dance. I was always one beat behind everyone, with my feet headed in the wrong direction.

Singing was my true joy. I often wake up in the morning still singing the hymn of praise that had filled my sleep. In church, when we lift our songs of love and praise, I see Christ tilting back his head in joyous laughter. Perhaps he sings with us. Song connects us to God. I certainly understand why the people of Angola filled their lives with the music of angels. They needed to stay strong and positive as they faced danger from their neighbors and the Portuguese. The Kingdom of Congo was allied with the Portuguese, yet Congo ruled over Angola.

Partial Christianization came to the people of the Congo in the early 1500s. Congo had also adopted the Portuguese language and some of their ways of dressing. Some in Angola, however, before the 1620s, had rejected the language of the Portuguese as well as their style of clothing as part of their resistance to the conquest by Portugal. Still, the influence of Portugal was growing in western areas of Angola near the border of Congo, as many of the Congolese were already adapting to European ways and customs.

After John Gowen left Africa, when Queen Nzinga Mbandi reigned (1624-1663), Portuguese culture and religion became more popular in Angola.

## Chapter Fourteen
### Portuguese Influence and Power

A Kimbundu-speaking Christian community existed in Angola by 1619. Some people were able to read and write Portuguese as early as 1491. It could be that the Angolans, bound for servitude or slavery in the New World, were Christians before they left Africa. Portugal's laws required the baptism of all enslaved Africans before arriving in the Americas. This religious rite meant a lot to the Portuguese. But did the Africans bring Christian practices, as we think of them? We don't know. We do know, they blended some religious practices of their native religion with the Roman Catholic religion of the Jesuits.

Whatever the reason for the baptism, the Angolans received new names before they boarded the ships. Many men and women who came on the first slave-ships in 1619 had Portuguese names given to them before they left Africa. Perhaps, many of the educated people had Portuguese names while they were still living in Angola.

## A Man of Significance

Education would have been a major part of the religious education offered by the Jesuits. With the religion of missionaries, education often came too. And with education came the Portuguese language and new names in Portuguese. Perhaps John was a baptized Christian. I based my assumption on the name of John Gowen's father, Dago Gonwelão — born in Congo in 1591 and died in 1691 in Bayern (now Bavaria), Germany, the place of his exile. John's grandmother was Nsaku Lau Dynasty (Dynasty Gomes Gomez) Gonwelao, and his grandfather, my nineth great-grandfather, was Portuguese (Portuguese Gomes Gomez) Gonwelao.

Since the Christian religion was in Angola for over one hundred years before slave traders loaded John Gowen and the other captives on the ships, they may have had Bible verses to comfort them during their Atlantic crossing.

> From Matthew 28:20, "And lo, I am with you always, even until the end of the world." (NIV)

> And Isaiah 41:13, "For I, the LORD your God, will hold your right hand, saying to you, 'Fear not, I will help you.'" (NIV)

John and the other 1619 captives could have included the memory of their deceased parents or grandparents as those who were strong in the world, despite adversity. I wondered who John may have held dear. Perhaps he had a favorite grandfather or granduncle.

John, and the other men, women, and children who survived the crossing, were sent to New Spain in 1619, where they were to work in the tobacco fields of Mexico or the mines of Brazil until they died. Why? Because

Portugal won the war in Angola, and part of the victory was Angola's ability to supply Portugal with enslaved people.

Europeans did not capture Africans for Virginia's tobacco fields in the following years, like those on the *White Lion* and *Treasurer*. Other Africans kidnapped the captives and then sold them to the captains of various slave-ships in the port of Luanda. As a result, those enslaved men and women who came after the 1619 group, and suffered the trip through the Middle Passage, usually came from different regions and villages of Africa. They spoke the language of their unique country and had dissimilar social, political, and religious customs.[17] The 1619 Angolan captives were different. They shared a complex ethnic identity since they all came from the same place.

With only a passing awareness of the slave trade, I looked up the term, the Middle Passage, to ensure I understood it.

The Middle Passage was the forced voyage of captured Africans across the Atlantic Ocean to the New World to be sold as enslaved people. It was considered a triangle-shaped route that shipped cargo, such as knives, guns, ammunition, cotton cloth, tools, and brass dishes, from Europe to Africa. The second leg was the nearly 7000-mile trip from Africa to the Americas and West Indies with a cargo of people. Leg three of the triangle was the trip back to Europe with the cargo of sugar, rice, tobacco, indigo, rum, and cotton from the Americas. The colonists had even produced silk and sent a gift of the delicate fabric back to King James. The voyage from Africa to the colonies took 21-to-90 days. Over three

## A Man of Significance

hundred years, slave traders pushed millions of African men, women, and children onto overcrowded sailing ships on which many died. The ships' crew were mostly from Great Britain, the Netherlands, Portugal, and France. [18]

After years of emissary trips from Angola to Portugal and aggression from Portugal on Angola, Portugal was still trying to seize Angola. Portugal didn't have enough workers in their country and desperately needed the labor of enslaved Angolans. Finally, they had help from hostile native bands near Angola to take the country.

Around 1600, Portuguese merchants working on the Angolan coast south of the Kwanza River encountered Imbangala bands ravaging the Kingdom of Benguela. John was born about 1605. His father, my eighth great-grandfather, Dago Gonwelão, could have seen the bands as a young man. These Imbangala marauders were prepared to sell captives they had stolen in their wars, to the Portuguese, in exchange for European goods.

The Imbangala took control of the Kwango Valley, forming a new kingdom. They expanded trade with neighbors in the region, sold salt for goods, and sold enslaved people to the Portuguese. Queen Nzinga of Angola (1582-1663) traveled to Luanda in 1623 and successfully negotiated for peace. The Portuguese administrator in charge of Angola adopted Nzinga as his goddaughter, giving her the Christian name Dona Ana de Souza.

Peace with Portugal, however, did not affect the poor relations between the Imbangala and Angolan kingdoms. The Imbangala continued attacking and kidnapping Angolan civilians, selling them into slavery. Portugal intervened militarily, supposably on Nzinga's behalf, and she and many Kimbundu retreated east to Matamba. Nzinga established a new Kimbundu kingdom and prepared for war with the Portuguese. The Portuguese declared Ari Kiluanji the new ngola (chief) as head of Angola. Kiluanji lacked political and religious legitimacy in the eyes of many Kimbundu who revolted against the new establishment with encouragement from Nzinga.

## Chapter Fifteen
### The Shaping of Your Ancestor's Country

Do some reading regarding the development of the country of your ancestor. Write a Timeline of the major events that shaped their development or lack of progress.

_____
_____
_____
_____
_____
_____
_____
_____
_____
_____
_____
_____
_____

_____

_____Add more pages as needed.

*Holy God, you are pure, creative love. I ask that you love and bless my family: those who went before and my family now, for all those in Heaven and on earth are yours. May anything I say, think, or do, not block their view of seeing you. I thank you for them, for you know the family I need and those who need me. In the name of Jesus, your son, I pray. Amen*
Or, write your own.

_____

_____

_____

_____

_____

_____

_____

Now write three things you're thankful for, because of your ancestor.

1._____

_____

2._____

_____

3._____

_____

## Chapter Sixteen
### Foods of Angola

For a diversion from war, let's warm our stomachs by turning to foods John might have eaten in Angola. There are many popular foods among Angolans and are also enjoyed by those who visit West Central Africa. I don't pretend to have eaten any of them, but I will try to find these foods in the United States and have a sample. I list them here by name, so you might look them up online or ask a friend about them. Some ingredients are familiar, and others are quite foreign to me.

Grandpa John isn't here so I can't ask him what meals his mother made. I would imagine he carried the taste and aroma of home in his memory all his life. We rarely forget smells or aromas. You may already know some foods, ingredients, and dishes listed here.

- Funge, made from the cassava or corn flour.
- Mukua sorbet.[19]

Doris Gaines Rapp, Ph.D.

When I researched the foods, many are the same foods we eat here in the United States. Basic foods such as beans and rice, pork, and the chickens John tended in their yard probably filled his mother's cooking pot. There are sauces and vegetables like onions and tomatoes. They also use spices such as garlic. Funge, a porridge made with cassava, is very popular. Portuguese cuisine greatly influenced Angolan cooking, like using olive oil and Piripiri, a local hot sauce.

Some of the prepared dishes that may have been on the Gowen table were:

- Fish Calulu, a typical dish from Angola and São Tomé e Principe. The fishing in Angola is fine with free meat for any meal.
- Mufete has grilled fish, plantain, sweet potato, cassava, and gari. Plantains are related to the banana family. Before they are ripe, they're yellow or green. When ripe, they're black. You can bake, boil, fry, grill, or steam them.
- Moamba de galinha, a traditional dish of Luanda, is made with palm oil, cassava flour porridge, okra, plantains, and wild spinach.
- Maize and cassava funge are typical side dishes in Angola.
- Feijão de óleo de palma is beans with palm oil and is another traditional dish of Angola.
- Moamba de galinha (chicken moamba) is chicken with palm paste, okra, garlic, and palm oil hash or red palm oil sauce, often served with rice and funge.
- Funge and moamba de galinha have been considered Angola's national dish.

## A Man of Significance

There are many other dishes, of course. I don't want to overwhelm you with foods that may be as new to you as they are to me. We can't say, "That would taste just like ...." We would have no taste memory for foods and dishes with different ingredients than we have used or eaten before. If you want to seek out Angolan foods, perhaps you can find a restaurant in a larger city near you that serves them. Let your server recommend dishes that you may like to try.

Fish stews are made with whatever is available and served with rice and muzongue. Muzongue is made from whole dried and fresh fish cooked with palm oil, sweet potato, onion, tomato, spinach, and spices and served with rice, spinach, *funje*, and farofa. Some Angolans believe the stew is a cure for a hangover if eaten before the onset of the headache.[20]

When enslaved Africans came to the New World, they brought their craving for certain foods with them. Perhaps some who remembered entire recipes came as early as Grandpa John. Don't forget; John Gowen was only fourteen years old when he was kidnapped from his homeland and sold as an unwilling indentured servant.

John was so young he would have just been starting his first year in high school if he had come to modern Virginia. We know what the captured ate on board that evil slave-ship, which was insufficient to sustain many of them. Or it was spoiled and unfit to eat. The Portuguese slave-ship, *San Juan Bautista*, began its journey across the ocean with 350 captured and enslaved Africans. Roughly 150 died en route, nearly half.

The frightened, homesick people probably longed for the tastes and familiar aromas from their mother's cooking stove. John could have dreamed of his family gathered at mealtime, eating baked chicken and rice. The crisp, brown skin of the chicken would have tasted perfect, and tantalized his taste buds.

The Angolans liked to chew on the kola nut for its caffeine. We like to drink it now in the form of Coca-Cola. The enslaved Africans brought their love of okra, watermelon, yams, black-eyed peas, and various peppers to the other side of the world. Do any of those foods sound familiar?

I had never eaten okra before we moved to the Mesilla Valley of New Mexico many years ago. Breaded and fried, it was wonderful. Be willing to try a new flavor. Life is about experiencing.

During the years of slavery, the plantation owner gave the enslaved people rations of food each week. A peck of cornmeal (two dry gallons or eight dry quarts) and three to four pounds of pork created the soul food staples of cornbread, fried catfish, barbecued ribs, chitterlings, and neckbones. [21] These foods became the savory memories of their new home.

I had never heard of cooked neckbones. Did John eat neckbones? The neck of what? I looked it up and found a traditional recipe cooked in today's method. The bones are the neckbones of pork, cooked very slowly. The modern "slow cooker" is ideal for cooking this special soul food. For neckbones, add onion, water or chicken broth, and various seasonings to four pounds of pork neckbones. A few minutes of preparation time, and then let them cook for four hours.

The diet of the enslaved, the middle class, and the wealthy was the same. What was different were the things added for flavor. During the colonial period, everyone ate corn cake. Families purchased sugar, butter, and spices to enhance the taste of the food as they had more money. They fried food, roasted, baked, grilled, and boiled foods. Does that sound like your kitchen or evenings in the yard around the BBQ grill? Colonial cooks even made ice cream.

During the 1700s, people ate pork, beef, lamb, fish, shellfish, and chicken. Vegetables from their garden included corn, beans, and other greens. Fruits from the trees and many types of baked goods concluded the meals. Corn, pork, and beef were staples in most lower and middle-class homes. They usually made a stew from these ingredients and served corn cake or corn pone with it. Corn pone is a thick, soft dough of cornmeal, water, and salt shaped into individual patties. They ate fish often since it was inexpensive or even free if they took their pole to the river. Fish and crab gave them protein and other nutritious elements.

As we know, "American food" is a blend of the foods from all the different cultures that immigrants, and in this case, enslaved people, brought with them when they came to this country. It shows that one of our melting pots is the pot on the back burner of our kitchen stove.

Enslaved people introduced slow-cooked stews, deep-frying techniques, and vegetarian dishes to the colonies. The ingredients for the new way of cooking included collard greens, peanuts, kidney and lima beans, rice, sorghum, millet, pineapple, chili peppers, sesame seeds, and the ingredients mentioned in the paragraphs above. If you are the cook at your house, you know how easy it is to prepare a one-pot stew dinner and let it slow-cook while you get computer work done, run the kids to practice, or play a game of tennis.

One food I've heard of and was curious about is the soul food, Chitterlings (Chitlins). [22] I looked up the recipe to get a general idea. Chitterlings, or chitlins, take an hour to prepare and three hours to cook. Chitterlings are pig intestines. Four pounds of fresh chitlins may be hard to find, but you could contact a local butcher. Add a large onion and red and green bell peppers to four pounds of chitterlings. A few of the other ingredients include celery and various seasonings. Add creole seasoning and red pepper flakes. **Eat chitlins with other soul foods like corn bread and greens.** Allow yourself an afternoon to make them, as cleaning them takes over half an hour to clean them properly. A spur-of-the-moment decision to fix chitlins won't get the food made. The word from the kitchen is that chitlins are very good.

Try a recipe from your family's culture. Go through your grandmother's recipe box and select a few recipes she served at Christmas and family gatherings. Many cooks from years ago jotted down a date in the corner of the card, referring to when they received the recipe. Your grandmother might have written a family name on the recipe, noting their preference. Have fun with these treasured keepsakes. You may not want to cook or bake the dish now, but you or your family may want to dig in with a spoon or fork sometime in the future. Enjoy.

## Chapter Seventeen
### Foods from Your Ancestor's Home of Origin

Each country, ethnicity, and family have a list of foods unique to their region. My recipe for date pudding is from another ancestor's line. It's been in the family for almost two hundred and fifty years. If you have no family recipes, google the traditional foods and dishes enjoyed in the country you are researching. On the lines below, write the names of the dishes that interest you. Or, make a note of the ones that are quite unusual. Write complete recipes on a three by five card and insert them in this book, or your recipe box, for future use.

_____

_____

_____

_____

_____

Doris Gaines Rapp, Ph.D.

_____

_____

*Holy God, you are pure, creative love. I ask that you love and bless my family: those who went before and my family now, for all those in Heaven and on earth are yours. May anything I say, think, or do, not block their view of seeing you. I thank you for them, for you know the family I need and those who need me. In the name of Jesus, your son, I pray. Amen*
Or, write your own.

_____
_____
_____
_____
_____
_____
_____
_____

Now write three things you're thankful for, because of your ancestor.
1._____

2._____

3._____

_____

## Chapter Eighteen
### Clothing of Ndongo/Angola

Each country seems to have its native costumes. Naturally, I was interested in the clothing of John Gowen's people of Angola in the early part of the seventeenth century. I wondered what John would have worn around home, feeding the farm animals, or hunting. Did his mother make his breeches? Did John stitch his own sandals or footwear? There are few pictures and illustrated articles of early Angolan clothing beyond the scantily clad warriors and hunters of wild game. I found two descriptions I'll pass on to you.

The first is a paragraph detailing an Angolan warrior in 1591. Filippo Pigafetta wrote about a memory he had of what Angolan warriors wore. You could sketch the warrior based on Pigafetta's description.

"On the head is a cap, crazily ornamented with the feathers of ostriches, peacocks, cockerels, and other birds, which makes the men seem taller and very frightening. Above the waist they are entirely

> naked, but they have iron chains with rings the size of a man's little finger, hanging down on each side to (the) right and left, which they wear for military pomp and display. Below the waist, they wear breeches of canvas or taffeta, and over them, a cloth that reaches down to their feet, with the folds turned back and tucked under the belt. This belt, as we have said, is of exquisite workmanship, with bells attached to it. On their legs, they wear boots similar to the laced boots of the Portuguese. We have already spoken of their weapons, which consist of bows, arrows, swords, daggers, and shields." [23]

That is a warrior's attire; a farmer's clothing would vastly differ from a warrior's. Still, let's look for a minute at what items the warrior had on. The feathers in the man's cap were from exotic birds in the area. Ostriches, peacocks, and cockerels have never flown into my backyard in midwestern United States or sat on the electric cables that run along the alley. The huge, thick loops of iron chain that hung down not only displayed the warrior's strength, but also the might of so great a country they were able to acquire, mold, and use the great resource of iron. Next, he described the breeches made of canvas, demonstrating an ability to weave. Taffeta is an important material, yet the warrior had access to the exotic fabric. The cloth that hung over his belt and down to the floor may have been woven in one of the native patterns of Angola, displaying his dedication and love for his country. His boots were in Portuguese style, indicating his link to a mighty European country and his

## A Man of Significance

willingness to adapt to modern ideas and times for his benefit.

Accessing a description of what Angolan women may have worn is limited to a few sentences about how the Angolan King's sister, Nzinga, adorned herself before an important meeting with the governor. Nzinga, dressed in her finest, complete with a crown on her head. A portrait of the Queen showed expensive fabrics from Europe draped from her shoulders. An Angolan necklace hung from her neck, displaying the wealth and power of the king. Another famous sketch of Nzinga when she met with the governor, doesn't quite display the same strength she usually presented.

The other sketch is well-known among those who have studied Angola's history and the strength of the women there. The other image is the actual 1622 meeting between Nzinga of Angola and the Portuguese governor, just three years after Portugal kidnapped John. Nzinga's brother, Ngola Mbande, was still the king of Angola in 1622. Ngola Mbande asked his sister to lead the delegation to meet with the Portuguese Governor of Angola, Joao Correia de Sousa.

Nzinga considered the clothes she wore to the meeting to be very important. Her garments could speak as clearly as her words. Nzinga was in the Portuguese-controlled city of Luanda in Angola, but she chose to wear the traditional royal dress of her culture rather than European attire. By 1622, the Portuguese had influenced the culture of Angola for many years, including clothing.

Nzinga wore "numerous cloths, jewels, and feathers in her hair" for the meeting. She brought other women, servants, and enslaved people dressed similarly, in more native attire. The picture of their meeting includes a servant carrying Nzinga's scepter, a symbol of power. Nzinga and her entourage made a dramatic entrance into the meeting, although the picture does not bear witness to the majesty of it all. The artist chose to downplay Nzinga's formidable appearance. For some reason, the artist left out some of the details of her attire, written about in historical documents. They did include the long, folded cloth that draped over one shoulder.

I loved Nzinga's strength and tenacity when she arrived at the meeting. The governor sat comfortably in the only chair in the room. That meant Nzinga had to

Fig 11. Nzinga before the Governor

stand before him as if she were subservient. However, she refused to be insulted. Calling one of her servants to kneel, Nzinga sat on the servant's back, using the servant as a human chair. When the meeting was over, Nzinga stood to leave. The Portuguese governor asked her about her servant, who still knelt on the floor. Nzinga answered

## A Man of Significance

the governor saying she planned to leave the servant there with the governor, since it was beneath her status to sit in the same chair twice.

This cleaver action revealed Nzinga's strength, power, and wealth, all important keys to her diplomatic role. She planned to convince the Portuguese not to continue invading and waging war against Angola. Sometimes actions like these convinced the governor to maintain a friendly relationship with the Matamba region to the east, where Nzinga was in power.[24]

After her brother's death, Nzinga became queen. A statue of the warrior queen, Queen Nzinga, was erected in Luanda in 1975 as an icon of resistance and independence. Angola finally became free of Portuguese rule after hundreds of years following the Angolan War of Liberation (1961-1974). Nzinga didn't dress in feathers and expensive cloths when she joined her warriors in the battle. To move easily, she wore a short skirt and a sleeveless top that would give her the freedom to wield a sword or dagger.

By contrast, the women of Colonial Jamestown, who greeted the *White Lion* in 1619, usually wore a two-piece dress. Actually, the few pieces of clothing that European women owned in the early 1600s, may have looked like the attire worn by the Portuguese women who lived in Angola.

Perhaps the two-piece dress was similar to a modern skirt and blouse, but in the 1600s, the top and bottom were of the same fabric, therefore, a dress. Under the skirt of the dress, an early settlement woman would wear a matching petticoat. The loose gown, or mantua, had a fitted bodice which was a sleeveless close-fitting waist-length garment that laced up the front, or a blouse with sleeves that came to the elbows. The full skirt may have had an opening in front that showed the petticoat beneath. Women of means wore similar clothing, but their gowns were of silk. Working-class women wore wool, cotton, or linen.

Wealthy women wore stays under their dresses, making their waists more defined and curvaceous. The stays the colonial women wore, later led to the corset. The early idea of stays was to correct posture. They were a band of linen with whalebone inside to create ribs.

The women wore mobcaps which were bonnets with a puffed crown and frilly gathering or lace around the face, at all times. As you can see from the rear view of this Williamsburg re-enactor on the left, they even wore the mobcaps under their hat while they were out. It reminded me of the little white hat Amish women wore in the plain communities we've lived in or nearby. Wealthy colonial women wore shoes of silk or leather with buckles across the top of their feet.

*Fig. 12 Williamsburg reenactor*

During colonial times, enslaved women would have worn less fancy but similar clothing. However, in the warm months, they may have worn no shoes.

# A Man of Significance

Men of all social classes in Jamestown during the seventeenth century, wore suits made of cotton, linen, wool, or leather. And those in service to them would be no different. The suit's coat was long and fell to the knees. The waistcoat was much longer than today's vest, and the fabrics used in the colonies were much less ornate. Still, if a community leader had brought a fancy waistcoat to Jamestown with him, he may have found a reason to wear it.

*Fig. 13 Leather Breeches*

Whatever John Gowen may have worn when captured, my guess is he would have worn that on the long voyage across the ocean, until he stepped onto the plantation of whoever bought John's indenture contract. Another guess would be, at some point he would have changed into the appropriate clothing befitting an English colonial resident, regardless of social status.

His pants, or breeches, were knee-length and could have been made of leather. As I thought about the deerskin, I thought it would make the over-the-knee pants heavy and hot. When I was in a shoemaker's shop in Historic Williamsburg, I took a picture of the leather breeches the cobbler had recently finished. They weren't heavy at all and were very soft.

Under the waistcoat, a man would have worn a long white linen shirt tucked into his breeches. George

Washington is wearing leather breeches in a well-known painting of him astride a horse.

Into the eighteenth century, men wore a cravat, a linen neckcloth. His shoes, made of soft leather, had straight soles worn on the right or left foot. The shoes closed with a top buckle. The cobbler had recently made the one on the right.

He said he made colonial shoes for all 485 workers at Historic Williamsburg.

*Fig. 14 Colonial shoe*

• • •

When my grandfather sold the farm, he made sure my husband, Bill, got the cobbler's bench out of the storage space upstairs. Originally, the house was an Ohio log cabin before previous ancestors added other rooms. When household items were no longer in use, they were put in the attic. The cobbler's bench was there, waiting to be rescued.

The lasts, for making shoes, were of several sizes, from small children to adults. Two of the lasts, the wooden forms that create the pattern around which the cobbler formed the leather, had straight, flat toes and did not have different tapers for the right or left foot.[25]

The picture of my grandfather's cobbler's bench with lasts and cobbler's tools, shows wooden shoe lasts in several sizes, boot lasts, the bench, and other equipment. The cobbler in Wilmington, Virginia, demonstrated his attempt to build up an existing last to fit the foot of another reenactor.

*Fig. 15 Cobbler's bench and tools*

## Chapter Nineteen
### The Traditional Clothing of Your Ancestor

Find the traditional clothing of the people of your ancestor's homeland. Place some examples here, or sketch the attire.

## A Man of Significance

*Holy God, you are pure, creative love. I ask that you love and bless my family: those who went before and my family now, for all those in Heaven and on earth are yours. May anything I say, think, or do, not block their view of seeing you. I thank you for them, for you know the family I need and those who need me. In the name of Jesus, your son, I pray. Amen*

Or, write your own.

_____
_____
_____
_____
_____
_____
_____
_____

Now write three things you're thankful for, because of your ancestor.

1._____
_____

2._____
_____

3._____
_____

## Chapter Twenty
### Family

    I will use my writing experience to plot a fictional scenario of John's possible family life and his African neighbors. A Portuguese visitor to Angola in the mid-1500s described the city of Angoleme as having 20,000 to 30,000 residents living in 5,000 to 6,000 thatched houses. Angoleme was the largest city at the time and perhaps the only city of any size in Angola. Most of the country was rural. I am guessing that the huts in many farming communities housed similar numbers of people.

    When I researched the Mbundu religion, I found that they highly respected their ancestors, even after those parents or grandparents were deceased. With their profound respect for family members, especially older people, several generations probably lived in the family home, whether a frame house or a hut. I don't know how large an Angolan hut was. My concept of the tiny, sparse space broadcasted on the news was to reveal extreme poverty. However, the people of Angola in the sixteenth and seventeenth centuries knew how to farm and construct buildings. They appeared to have been an industrious people.

The weather in Angola, "is tempered by a cool sea current along the coast and by the altitude in the plateau which is found in the interior." Those elements create a sub-tropical climate in nearly the entire country. Angola's winter begins at varied times, as expected in a country that covers a huge space. From May to August is the austral winter, or southern hemisphere winter, when it's cool and dry (Cacimbo). The austral summer arrives at differing times, from mid-September to April in the northeast, mid-October to April in the center, and November to March in the south. Along the coastal area, summer is from February to April in Luanda. The rainy season is almost non-existent on the southern coast, which makes it a desert.[26]

The sub-tropical climate of Angola would make for easy living inside and out. Perhaps John's family cooked in the open in a horno-type bake oven. Maybe he had sisters who helped with chopping vegetables, while John and his father hunted for deer or took their poles to the water's edge.

Native Americans in the Southwest United States baked in a similar structure used in Angola, a kiva oven, made of adobe-mud. Bricks are created by filling wooden molds with a mix of red, adobe clay. The bricks are laid out in the sun to dry. The oven, shaped like a large beehive, is covered with more adobe-mud, and left to harden in the southwestern sun. Cooking outside is like our open-concept homes of today, with everyone gathered around in the kitchen during food preparation.

I think of John Gowen's extended family, perhaps all living under the same roof. Amish homes in Elkhart and Adams counties of Indiana, also stretch out in several directions to make room for newly married adult children and their families.

John's home may have been full of parents, grandparents, brothers, and sisters. I don't know how many children were in an African family four hundred years ago. Based on the number of those living in each household in 1564, maybe many children were born to parents.

Can you see small children at play in the warm weather chasing the Angolan white lady butterfly or the beautiful blue morpho? Can't you see the family along the ocean's edge on the Atlantic side of the country, enjoying the warm water, the salt air, and the brilliant sun? Aunts, uncles, and cousins perhaps lived next door or down the lane.

I can relate to John's large family. As I've said, my mother was an only child, but Dad was one of six children. He had two sisters and three brothers. Family closeness is like a security blanket, wrapped around you safely and warmly throughout life. Parents, aunts, and uncles teach life lessons.

Imagine the deep and lasting pain of being ripped from your parents and a very large family at age fourteen, just as you inhaled the new experiences of being a man. We know even now, having your familiar male role models around during the teen years is very important. Mothers nurture young children. Fathers prepare them for life beyond home when they are teens. If Dad isn't there, other strong male role models must guide them, and walk with them into adulthood.

At John's age, he would have hunted with arrow and spear by his age at capture, cleaned the hides, and butchered the meat. The Angolan family usually raised small animals like chickens, sheep, and pigs. It would probably have been John's responsibility to feed the animals and tend to their needs. Who wouldn't love to care for woolly ones, like the sheep below?

Fig. 16 Picture contributed by Rachel Marie Hester

John may have had excellent training and experience raising sheep for wool. His mother at home, or the women in the colonies, would spin the sheep's wool into yarn. Caring for the pigs and cows trained him, while he still lived in Angola, for the litter of piglets he would raise later.

Fig. 17 Picture contributed by Rachel Marie Hester

Given the years of war and unrest in Angola, the stoic response to possible military injury would have been learned before age fourteen. Training in military skills was probably experienced by all the young men. The slave trade was already well established. Captains of slave-ships sold enslaved people to European countries, New Spain (Mexico), and other countries in South America.

By contrast, a fourteen-year-old boy would have experienced years of childhood training. Their entire family would probably have been home every day. A young boy would have shadowed their father, and a girl their mother. Big brothers and sisters would have helped nurture and train their younger siblings.

The evening might have been story time with parents and grandparents telling the tales of generations from long ago. Grandpas could have praised an ancestor's bravery. They might have shared humorous, daily experiences of distant relatives that could bring laughter to the children. An evening with everyone at home is a rare experience in today's families. The Angolan family life, four hundred years ago, was predictable, dependable, together, and therefore safe.

Vacillation between the other side of their "normal" lives of family and safety, and the many waring attacks, were also part of their lives.

The thought of John's entire world turned upside-down when he was seized and removed from his home, is gut-wrenching. The kidnapping would have shaken him until his balance was rattled and forced through a sieve of life where nothing that had been was anymore.

## Chapter Twenty-One
### Family Life in Your Ancestor's Home

Are there any customs in the family life of your ancestor that are interesting and unique to their country? Write them here.

_____
_____
_____
_____
_____
_____
_____
_____
_____
_____
_____
_____
_____

Doris Gaines Rapp, Ph.D.

_____

_____

*Holy God, you are pure, creative love. I ask that you love and bless my family: those who went before and my family now, for all those in Heaven and on earth are yours. May anything I say, think, or do, not block their view of seeing you. I thank you for them, for you know the family I need and those who need me. In the name of Jesus, your son, I pray. Amen*
Or, write your own.

_____
_____
_____
_____
_____
_____

Now write three things you're thankful for, because of your ancestor.

1._____

2._____

3._____

_____

## Chapter Twenty-Two
### Girls

Perhaps more complicated than the war strategy would have been the relationships involved in courting. The presence of fathers and other men of quality would have been vital to John Gowen's development. As young boys follow their fathers into the hunting grounds, farming fields, and village construction, they learn to be strong, honest, loyal, and loving men. A boy might grow into a fatherless man without that bonding and apprentice opportunity. Depression and suicide are two outcomes that happen more often in families with absent fathers. Fatherless men can be unstable, easily angered, and untrusting of the world around them.

We know that John Gowen was not fatherless. His father was living when Portugal invaded their country, seizing John. We are sure of that because the research showed that Dago Gonwelão was born in Luanda, Angola, then called Kabasa. He was the father of John Gowen. As stated, Dago died in 1691 in Bayern (Bavaria), Germany, seventy-two years after John's kidnapping.

In present-day America, a fourteen-year-old would begin their first year of high school at the age the kidnappers tore John's life apart. Girls would have caught a boy's eye by now. In our country, kids attracted to one another might agree to meet on the third bleacher, center section, of a high school ball game or gather some friends and attend a movie together. Unable to legally drive, they would depend on their normal routine to find time and places to spend together.

John Gowen probably didn't have a school building with end-of-the-day activities, but we can all be sure that kids began to test the waters of dating by age fourteen. Today, group activity is fun. Would the social morays of Angola have required a chaperone to accompany the young people? Would social etiquette have forbidden them from being alone together?

If he were introduced to a girl's family, the custom in Angola would have been for John to greet the elders first. He would also bow to older family members. In the countryside, women and girls traditionally don't look another person in the eyes. Young Angolans today, and those living in large cities like Luanda, reject the custom of not making eye contact.

As we all know, whatever the customs, nothing would keep young people from pairing up. Practicing the courting ritual until one finds the person that seems to fit has been a major part of life since life began.

The odds are, by the time they kidnapped John, he had a special girl in his life. I could not find the age of marriage for the young people in Angola during the very

## A Man of Significance

early 1600s, so we won't stretch our thinking that far. John may have left his family, his friends, and a girlfriend when the warriors carried him off into captivity.

The connection between two who are falling in love is even stronger than the ties with family members. That's why they leave their family and travel around the world to help another or find their love.

John may have been torn from his homeland, leaving a girlfriend behind. One can grieve a lifetime over the loss of a love.

When we think of the other Angolans who made the life-threatening trip across the ocean with John, do we think of them as real people with families, loving relationships, and a future to plan and look forward to? It was hundreds of years ago, but we can't dismiss them as statues or framed portraits. John and a girlfriend would have spent time together or had a marriage arranged for them with no pre-planning.

If John left a new love behind, would he have compared each new woman he met to one he'd never see again? How much more did John lose, or leave behind, when he left for the New World?

## Chapter Twenty-Three
**Courting Practices**

In your research on the customs of courting in the country your ancestor was from, what did you find that was unique to their culture? Are there any funny or interesting stories? Write them here.

_____
_____
_____
_____
_____
_____
_____
_____
_____
_____
_____

## A Man of Significance

*Holy God, you are pure, creative love. I ask that you love and bless my family: those who went before and my family now, for all those in Heaven and on earth are yours. May anything I say, think, or do, not block their view of seeing you. I thank you for them, for you know the family I need and those who need me. In the name of Jesus, your son, I pray. Amen*

Or, write your own.

_____

_____

_____

_____

_____

_____

_____

_____

Now write three things you're thankful for, because of your ancestor.

1._____

_____

2._____

_____

3._____

_____

## Chapter Twenty-Four
### Villages and Language

Today, Luanda it is a large port city on the northern coast. It is a blend of Portuguese-style colonial landmarks and traditional African housing. But when Grandpa John lived there, I read that the structures were primitive.

However, even all of those years ago, Portugal had made some changes in the culture of Angola. Long before John Gowen was a child, most people spoke Portuguese with a blend of native words. By 1491, some of the indigenous Angolan groups could also read Portuguese. Some people, however, refused to speak Portuguese, rebelling against the European country's interference in their country. I'm guessing that many Angolan groups were more educated than we may have previously guessed. The commoners certainly had privileges that others didn't.

Having lived in many areas of Indiana, the blended languages in Angola remind me of some friends. In some areas of the Hoosier state, the Amish mix their Swiss language with the English they live and work with. Some children in those families, who haven't learned to separate English from Swiss, are hard to understand as the two languages jumble together.

Angolans finally chose their way of speaking. They spoke, and still do speak, the Bantu language of the people in the Niger-Congo language family. Those people live in Africa's western, central, and southern parts. The largest group in that population is the Ovimbundu. They speak Umbundu and represent one-fourth of that population.

That area of Africa has a very ancient history. Archeologists have found that the earliest people in the Congo were there in the Paleolithic Period, also called the Old Stone Age, at least 80,000–90,000 years ago. Ancient tools found in the area determined those dates. Between 2000 BC and 500 AD, Bantu migrations came into the basin from the northwest. They brought agriculture, iron-making techniques from West Africa, and the Bantu Language family. The indentured servants and enslaved people who came to Jamestown in 1619 brought those skills to the colonies.

We can't read about the country by opening the doors to ancient libraries, because there weren't any in Angola. Written knowledge of the country was nonexistent and, therefore, unavailable for research. The early people of Angola left no written records of their history. There is no precious Tora or a Qumran cave hiding place full of dead sea scrolls. All the Angolans had was an oral history.

Think of stories you have heard and shared of your family and friends around the fire pit in the backyard on a warm summer evening. That is what the people of

Angola had, to give them knowledge of where they came from and what their people had experienced. The Kingdom of Angola's first recorded or written history was in the 1500s.

As has been stated, the country of Angola was a vassal state of Congo, although Angola was more powerful. A vassal state is a country or "state with varying degrees of independence in its internal affairs but dominated by another state in its foreign affairs and potentially wholly subject to the dominating state."[27] The Angolan king was called the Ngola. That was where the Portuguese got the name Angola.

In the late 1500s, the Jesuit Baltasar Barreira sailed to Angola and collected some of the country's oral traditions. He described the founder of the kingdom, Ngola Kiluanje, known as Ngola Inene, as a migrant and chief of the Kimbundu-speaking ethnic people. [28]

While on first reading, many words and names in their language are difficult to pronounce. Still, they are interesting to roll over your tongue as you proceed. To pronounce more correctly, go to www.howtopronounce.com.

## Chapter Twenty-Five
### Your Family's Language

What was the language of your ancestor's homeland? Are you surprised? Did you learn that language in high school or college? Did your family speak the language in your home when you were growing up? Use these prompts to help you find some interesting facts.

How was your ancestor's name pronounced? You can google it and write it phonetically.

_____

How would your name have been pronounced?

_____

Look up these phrases in case you ever go to that country:

Take me to the hotel.

_____

Where is the restroom?

_____

Doris Gaines Rapp, Ph.D.

Where is a restaurant?
_____

And, the sentence everyone wants to learn: I love you.
_____

Other words you might like to learn:
_____

_____

Add a few sentences you would find useful:
_____

_____

_____

_____

_____

_____

_____

_____

*Holy God, you are pure, creative love. I ask that you love and bless my family: those who went before and my family now, for all those in Heaven and on earth are yours. May anything I say, think, or do, not block their view of seeing you. I thank you for them, for you know the family I need and those who need me. In the name of Jesus, your son, I pray. Amen*

Or, write your own.

_____
_____
_____
_____
_____
_____
_____

Now write three things you're thankful for, because of your ancestor.

1._____
_____

2._____
_____

3._____
_____

# Chapter Twenty-Six
## Growth and Development of the Virginia Colony

Fig. 18 Jamestown Settlement 1619

England's King James I, granted the first Charter of Virginia, on April 10, 1606. The Virginia Company of

## A Man of Significance

London, and the people they found to invest in the company, were permitted to settle a large strip of the North American coast. The London-based company established Jamestown the next year, in 1607. [30]

Originally, one hundred and four English men and boys arrived in North America from England very early in the seventeenth century. The investors selected the site at Jamestown for the settlement on May 13, 1607, because it met the criteria of the Virginia Company, which funded the establishment of the settlement. To protect the settlement from the Spaniards, whose ships sailed up and down the coast, ready to attack; the spot had to be inland, far enough not to be seen from the Atlantic Ocean. Those assigned to select a proper site, sailed up the James River to Point Comfort. The Jamestown settlement became the first permanent English settlement in North America.

*Fig. 19 The James River*

After the men constructed the fort, they invited women to leave England and come to Virginia to provide the stability for Jamestown to survive. The women would add all the long hours of work that happened in any home in colonial times, from washing over the washboard, to spinning and weaving fabric. Females would also provide the warmth and nurturance added to a community. A colony of families was the expected outcome. Above is the meeting house at Jamestown.

*Fig. 20 Jamestown Settlement*

The first women in Virginia arrived in 1608, with many more that followed throughout the next few years. Lord Bacon, a member of the Council for Virginia on behalf of King James I, said in1620, "When a plantation grows to strength, then it is time to plant with women as well as with men; that the plantation may spread into generations, and not be ever pieced from without."[31]

The English men and women were here for twelve years, building their settlement, tending gardens, and planting tobacco before the "Jamestown twenty and odd" African indentured servants and enslaved people inadvertently landed on their shore. Building a community out of the raw wilderness was hard for the Europeans who weren't used to manual labor and had few building skills. They had to quickly learn the "mud and stud, post construction" of the colonial buildings. The English who had come to the new Colony were often the second or third non-inheriting son of a wealthy Englishman. They came to the New World to make their fortune. They were hardly the type of people one would imagine would want to live in a new colony built out of nothing but hard, physical labor. The arrival of the Angolans brought knowledge of farming and construction and helped save the Virginia Colony. The Angolans had all the skills the English lacked to survive in the wilderness. Some buildings were stick framed, like the fences.

*Fig. 21 Mud and Stud Construction*

*Fig. 22 Stick Framing*

Doris Gaines Rapp, Ph.D.

*Fig. 23 & 24 Inside Governor Delaware's home Williamsburg*

There were many ways in which the New World grew. As part of the country's development, a court system was established based on the courts of England. The Colony's development of legal representation included a sheriff in addition to judges. The Legislature even developed courts on the local level.

The Pilgrims landed in 1620 and started the Plymouth Colony. Travel was hard between Jamestown, Plymouth, and other Colonies, and could be dangerous. So, the Inferior Courts, which were local, were established due to a demand for an extension of the judiciary. By 1632, they had created a monthly court located on the eastern side of the Chesapeake Bay, along with two additional Inferior Courts.

Muster roles or censuses of the time revealed written documentation attesting to the Colony's growth. When the colony's assembly met in July and August 1619, they made plans to reconvene on March 1, 1620. It may have been because of that meeting that they compiled demographic data on the Virginia Colony's population. By March 1620, a census revealed that there were 892 European colonists living in Virginia, with males outnumbering females by nearly seven to one. Also present were 32 Africans (17 women and 15 men) and four "Indians," who, like the Africans, were described as being "in ye service of severall planters." It is still uncertain where these men and women were living. Some probably were on Jamestown Island with Sir George Yeardley and Captain William Peirce as they originally purchased the Angolans who arrived in 1619, and those households had African servants four years later. In March 1620, the Virginia colonists had a supply of livestock and military equipment and 222 "habitable houses," not counting barns and storehouses. There were 117 people in James City, Jamestown Island, and on the mainland, the colony's most populated area. Listed were 84 men, 24 women, 9 children, and 112 cattle (9 oxen and one bull that belonged to the public and 22 bulls and 80 kine [cows] that belonged to private individuals). Some may have been on the lower side of the James River, at Hog Island, a short distance across the water. [32]

    1634 — The Virginia Colony was divided into eight shires — or counties — like the shires of England. Court was to be held once a month in the shire. As they organized new counties, they gave each a local court.

    1658 — By 1658, there were sixteen shires in Virginia.

    1671 — In 1672, the number increased to twenty shires.

1699 — Twenty-two shires were present in 1671.

1714 — Fifteen years later, the New World had grown to twenty-five shires.

1782 — By 1782, there were seventy-four shires.

From early in the development of the court system, the Act of 1624 provided that the judges of the monthly courts, which were the local ones, should be "the commanders of the places and such others as the governor and council shall appoint by commission." Those early judges were known as commissioners of the monthly courts, then as justice of the peace. The office of justice of the peace, or magistrate, was one of dignity. He was a respected man of the community with influence and ability.

Very few magistrates had trained in the law, and many had little general education. A "Justice in Colonial Virginia county courts didn't involve difficult points of law, and, therefore, the sound judgment and good common sense of the justices must in a large measure have compensated for their lack of legal knowledge."[33]

The jurisdiction of the county courts was in both civil and criminal cases. I found it interesting that once a year, the Justice of the Peace investigated the management of the estates of orphans and fatherless children who were bound out and had no property. They also made sure that orphan-apprentices were treated properly and received an education. The court's jurisdiction in civil cases increased, covering larger amounts of property and money, from one hundred pounds of tobacco to sixteen pounds sterling, or sixteen hundred pounds of tobacco. If a litigant didn't follow through with the amount the court awarded, the magistrate was authorized to imprison him.

Magistrates even heard the complaints of servants who weren't treated properly by their owners. If evidence proved the charges were true, the planter would stand before the magistrate for judgment.

According to geni.com, at some point, Grandpa John Gowen, the first free man of color in the colonies, was assigned an additional responsibility to his many job titles — "magistrate, auditing, and ruling over smaller filings. In York County, in his later years, John judged Europeans and Africans alike until his death."

As the Negro enslaved population grew, the Legislator wrote a law stating that a Black man could no longer sit in judgment over an Englishman. However, they didn't enact the law until after John Gowen died. To me, that shows the people's respect for John's honesty, ability, and common sense in using the law correctly. John Gowen was indeed a man of significance.

## Chapter Twenty-Seven
### Growth of Your Ancestor's Homeland

We have seen how the Virginia Colony grew. As the population and territory expanded, more counties or shires pushed into the wilderness. To narrow your research:

    Focus on the town your ancestor came from, rather than the entire country.

    Look at their population growth or decline.

    Make a notation to explain the changes, like a new industry moved in, or closed, perhaps relocated to another community.

_____
_____
_____
_____
_____

_____ Add more pages as needed.

*Holy God, you are pure, creative love. I ask that you love and bless my family: those who went before and my family now, for all those in Heaven and on earth are yours. May anything I say, think, or do, not block their view of seeing you. I thank you for them, for you know the family I need and those who need me. In the name of Jesus, your son, I pray. Amen*
Or, write your own.

_____

_____

_____

_____

_____

_____

_____

_____

Now write three things you're thankful for, because of your ancestor.

1._____

2._____

3._____

## Chapter Twenty-Eight
### Freedom

John Gowen's name at birth, João Geaween, sounds Portuguese, but he was not European. He was African.

I smiled as I thought of the old, one-drop rule that people, only in the United States, lived under. Based on the "one-drop rule," many years ago, I may have been considered Black, even though I don't have a single drop of Black blood. No other country followed the "one-drop" way of labeling people. The old "rule" was clear. If someone had even one distant relative of Black ancestry, one drop of African blood, they were considered Black.

The one-drop rule was a legal principle to classify people according to race. Some states even made it law as late as the early twentieth century. Mixed-race children were considered the race of the group believed to have a lower status. With the One-Drop Rule, those in control tried to prevent interracial marriage and attempted to deny Blacks their rights and equal opportunities. It wasn't until 1967, that the Supreme Court outlawed the One-Drop Rule.[34]

When we consider the Melungeon people I began to describe in Chapter Four, we may wonder if the tri-racial group was discriminated against more or less than bi-racial people. It is so hard for me to understand why any group of people created by the living God could be considered less than others. We are all one in Him.

The Melungeon family tree began with John and Margret Gowen in the English settlement of Jamestown in British Colonial America. Yes, our John Gowen. The plot of their drama began like a romantic movie with a familiar love triangle. Over thousands of years, how many lives have been destroyed by infidelity?

We know that John Gowen was an African-indentured man and the servant of the Englishman, William Evans. John was one of the prisoners on the Portuguese ship, *São João Bautista,* when it was attacked, stopped, and boarded by the English pirate, Captain Arthur Guy. Captain Guy turned north, sailed for the Virginia colony, and traded his stolen Angolan captives in Jamestown for tobacco and other needed supplies. These were the first enslaved people in North America. But a slave market was not yet in place in the new colony. However, the English knew about indentured servants since the indentured system existed in England for many years.

Fig. 25 Sailing ship - Jamestown

When my husband and I were in Virginia, I snapped the photo to the left of a sailing ship moored at the reconstructed fort of the Jamestown settlement. See how small the ships were that crossed the ocean during the 1600s.

When the *White Lion* arrived at Point Comfort, Sir George Yeardley, Virginia's Governor, and Abraham Peirsey, the colony's Cape Merchant, placed a bid with the ship's captain on behalf of the colony. It was Peirsey's job to buy supplies for the colony. Today, some still debated whether the colony representatives bought the Angolans as enslaved people or indentured servants. We'll discuss that debate in other sections of the book.

The *White Lion* left Point Comfort, sailed to Jamestown, and docked. The Muster rolls are fuzzy at this point. In a paper written by Beth Auston, the Registrar and Historian of the Hampton History Museum, *1619: Virginia's First Africans,* Auston wrote: "In March 1620 the captives were still listed, 'in the service of several plantations.'" Either William Evans offered a bid for John Gowen in Jamestown, or John continued to be owned by Yeardley and worked on Evans' plantation. If John were indentured, his service would have been about 7-10 years. John probably worked for Evans in his tobacco fields as a field hand. He was still not a free man of color in 1641 when he was described in a lawsuit as "John Gowen, being a negro servant unto William Evans."

# A Man of Significance

"One example of the treatment of black workers as servants is demonstrated by the case of John Graweere, a servant to William Evans. In 1641, Graweere was permitted by Evans to 'keep hogs.' Graweere was to provide 'half the increase' to Evans and could keep the other half 'for his own benefit.'" [35]

The passage just quoted is a documented statement that Evans gave John Gowen permission to raise hogs on a small plot of land. As stated, from the sale of the pigs, John was to divide the earnings with Evans. John must have been a man with a clear focus and some business skills. "John Gowen served his indenture time as a servant/slave for planter Williams Evans" [36] and was North America's first, or one of the first, recorded free Black man.

William Evans' neighbor, Robert Sheppard, owned the Chippoke plantation in Surry County. Lt. Sheppard was also one of the top leaders of the Virginia colony and served in the Virginia House of Burgess, North America's oldest continually existing legislature.

Margaret Cornish, my seventh great-grandmother, enslaved by Robert Sheppard, lived on Sheppard's nearby plantation. Together John and Margaret produced a son. Five years later, on March 31, 1641, John purchased the freedom of that son from Lt. Robert Sheppard when Margaret Cornish became pregnant by Robert Sweat, a neighbor, while still married to John Gowen.

Some say enslaved people like Margaret couldn't get married. Remember, Margaret may not have been "enslaved" since the first Angolans were probably indentured. I'll refer back to the Colonial Records of Virginia 1619-1680, first introduced in Chapter Two, regarding the colony's first servitude. That early colonial document stated that a "maid or woman servant, either now residing in the colony or hereafter to come, shall contract herself in marriage without either the consent of her parents, or of her master or mistress, or of the magistrate and minister of the place both together."

The Virginia Court on October 17, 1640, handed down Margaret's and Robert's sentences.

The Virginia General Assembly censured the couple for fornication on October 17, 1640. Fornication is intimate relations with a married person. Margaret was still married to John Gowen. When Margaret and the White man, Sweat, were brought before the court, it wasn't because races couldn't mingle. Their charge was fornication. Margaret and John Gowen would have had to be married to bring a conviction of fornication.

Margaret Gowen and Robert Sweat were judged guilty as charged. The Virginia court records contained the following sentence:

"Whereas Robert Sweat hath begotten with child a negro woman servant belonging unto Lieutenant Sheppard, the court hath therefore ordered that the said negro woman shall be whipt at the whipping post and the said Sweat shall tomorrow in the forenoon do public penance for his offense at James City Church in the time of divine service according to the laws of England in that case provided." [37]

Sweat's punishment was to wear a white robe to church during worship the next day, a judgment used by the English in the past. It was the humiliation that was to cause emotional pain. Although about five months pregnant, Margaret Cornish Gowen was whipped at the town whipping post. It is obvious the punishment was not equal.

Within five months of his wife and Robert Sweat's sentence, John Gowen petitioned the court for custody of his and Margaret's son, five-year-old Mihill. The date of the suit would have coincided with the time Margaret may have given birth to her child by Robert Sweat.

On March 31, 1641, John Gowen brought the following suit:

> *"Whereas it appeareth to the court that John Gowen, being a negro servant unto William Evans, was permitted by his said master to keep hogs and make the best benefit thereof to himself provided that the said Evans might have half the increase which was accordingly rendered unto him by the said negro and the other half reserved for his own benefit: And whereas the said negro having a young child of a negro woman belonging to Lt. Robert Sheppard which he desired should be made a Christian and he taught and exercised in the church of England, by reason whereof he, the said negro did for his said child purchase its freedom of Lt. Sheppard with the good liking and consent of Tho. Gooman's overseer, as by the deposition of the said Sheppard and Evans appeareth, the court hath therefore ordered that the child shall be free from the said Evans or his assigns and to be and remain at the disposing and education of the said Gowen and the child's godfather who undertaketh to see it brought up in the Christian religion as aforesaid."* [38]

John Gowen desired to raise his son as a Christian within the Church of England. John also wanted Mihill to receive an education, as stated in the court petition, that his son "be taught and exercised in the church of England."

John Gowen won his court case. The court also stated, "The child was not to be a servant or slave to Evans or others" since John was still a servant in the home of Evans.

"Graweere's (Gowen's) successful petition to purchase his child indicates another difference between white and black men. Graweere's decision to use the court to secure his son's freedom indicates that he was one of the many blacks in Virginia who knew how to use the colony's institutions." [39]

In some research, John Gowen was said to understand the social underpinnings in his community. Many early Blacks in the colonies had "exhibited a sure-handed understanding of Chesapeake social hierarchy and the complex dynamics of patron-client relations." [40]

At some point, John Gowen remarried. I could find no records of his second wife's name or the date of their marriage. Articles did report John and his new wife had at least one son named Philip, born about 1650.

Margaret and Robert Sweat remained together. Whether others knew they were still a couple is unknown, but Margaret was no longer married to John Gowen. So, fornication was not a problem. And, at that time, there were no laws against Blacks and Whites being together. Besides her first child that brought the whipping, Margaret had another child with Sweat out of wedlock. Both children had Margaret's original surname, Cornish.

A Man of Significance

Others in the small community would certainly have been aware that she and Sweat were still a couple when she had her second son. Much later, Margaret Cornish was freed but did not free herself from the land. She lived the rest of her life on a section of Sheppard's plantation called Hod Island.

The names of Gowen, Sweat, and Cornish remain a part of the Melungeon tree of descendants, African, White, and Native American, to this day. [41] According to Ancestry DNA, my Gaines line goes back to them.

John Gowen & Margaret Cornish
▼ (Margaret & Robert Sweet had children.)

Mihill Gowen & Prossa///    Mihill Gowen & a white woman
▼                                    ▼
William Gowen               Thomas Christopher
                                         "Sobering Wind" Gowen
                                         (Part Cherokee) &
                                         Winona Dakota
                                         WinuNna Cherokee Indian
                                                   ▼
                                         Richard Gowen/Gaines
                                         (Wh/Afr/Cherok)
                                         & Catherina Rawlings
                                         Madison
                                                  ▼
                                         Richard M. Pendleton Gaines
                                         & Mildred Hollinger
                                                  ▼
                                         Daniel George Gaines &
                                         Catherine (Katy) Lee Gaines
                                                  ▼
                                         Daniel Harry Gaines &

Doris Gaines Rapp, Ph.D.

>Jenny Lee
>▼
>William Melvin Gaines &
>Josie Davis
>▼
>Daniel Morton Gaines &
>Mildred Marie Bryson
>▼
>Doris Jean Gaines Rapp

    John Gowen and his family's experiences with the court brought notice to his wise judgment. John's life started much differently than it ended. A kidnapped young man from Africa, moved to the other side of the world from his home and family, became a trusted and respected free man in Colonial America. He was a man of significance.

## Chapter Twenty-Nine
### Event(s) in the Life of Your Lost One

What events have you uncovered through research, talking to family members or others, that revealed some reasons for your ancestor's behavior? Write some notes on these lines.

_____
_____
_____
_____
_____
_____
_____
_____
_____
_____
_____

Doris Gaines Rapp, Ph.D.

*Holy God, you are pure, creative love. I ask that you love and bless my family: those who went before and my family now, for all those in Heaven and on earth are yours. May anything I say, think, or do, not block their view of seeing you. I thank you for them, for you know the family I need and those who need me. In the name of Jesus, your son, I pray. Amen*
Or, write your own.

_____

_____

_____

_____

_____

_____

_____

_____

Now write three things you're thankful for, because of your ancestor.

1. _____

_____

2. _____

_____

3. _____

_____

## Chapter Thirty
### Second Generation:
### Mihill (Michael) Gowen, Son of John Gowen

Since Mihill Gowen was my sixth great-grandfather, I want to tell you a little about him. Mihill was five years old when his father, John Gowen, won the lawsuit over his wife, Margaret Cornish. The suit gave John custody of their son. In 1641, John placed Mihill in the home of Captain Christopher Stafford, as an indentured servant, on the York County plantation, Martin's Hundred. Mihill's name, and later Mihill's son, appears in Ivor Noël Hume's book, *Martin's Hundred,* as residents of that plantation. This indentured arrangement for Mihill ensured that someone else would not be able to capture and sell him. As important to John, Mihill would receive an education, and John and Stafford would raise him as a Christian in the Church of England. Mihill was to remain a servant in the Stafford family until he was eighteen.

However, Christopher Stafford died before Mihill's eighteenth birthday. Stafford's sister, Amy Stafford

Barnhouse, then legally held Mihill's indenture through inheritance. Take a moment and notice that her name is Amy. Poor spelling has it written several ways in the same colonial document.

Barnhouse also had an African American servant girl named "Prossa." When Mihill lived at Martin's Hundred, he and Prossa had a child whom they named William Gowen.

In his will, Captain Stafford wanted Mihill freed from servitude upon Stafford's death. His sister carried out his wishes on October 25, 1657. Amy Barnhouse gave a legal statement also freeing Mihill's two-year-old son William, but she retained the child's mother, Prossa, as her servant, which broke up the family.

> "Bee itt known unto all Christian people that whereas Mihill Gowen Negro of late servant to my Brother Xopher Stafford deced by his last will & Testament bearing Date the 18 of Jan 1654 had his freedom given unto him after the expiration of 4 years-service unto my uncle Robert Stafford. Therefore know all whom itt may concern that I Anne Barnehouse for divers good couses mee hereunto moving do absolutely quitt & discharge the sd Mihill Gowen from any service & for ever sett him free from any claim of service either by mee or any one my behalf as any part or parcell of my Estate that may be claimed by mee the said Amy Barnhouse my heyres Exers Admrs or Assignes as witness my hand this 25 Oct 1657 Amy (AB) Barnhouse Bee itt knowne unto all Xcian people that I Ame Barnehouse of Martins

hundred widdow for divers good causes & consideracons mee hereunto moving hath given unto Mihill Gowen Negro he being att this time servant unto Robert Stafford a Male child borne the 25 August 1655 of the body of my Negro Prosta being baptised by Mr. Edward Johnson 2 Sept 1655 & named William & I the said Amy Barnhouse doth bindmy selfe my heyres Exer Admr & Ass never to trouble or molest the said Mihill Gowin or his sone William or demand any service of the said Mihill or his said sone William In witnes whereof I have caused this to be made & done I hereunto sett my hand & Seale this present 16 Sept 1655 Amy (AB) Barnhouse."

John Gowen and his immediate family certainly knew how to use the judicial system of seventeenth-century colonial America. Another of John's sons, Philip Gowen, successfully sued for his freedom on June 16, 1675, from John Lucas. "The General Court (of Virginia) orders the black indentured servant Phillip Gowen to be freed, finding that his master cheated him." [42]

The planter, Lucas, was ordered to provide the "Negro" Phillip with "three Barrels of Corne att the Cropp" according to the will of Amy Beazley, Phillip Gowen's original mistress. According to some researchers, several African American Gowens left court and land documents from seventeenth-century Virginia.

After Mihill's release from servitude to the Staffords, he quickly remarried a free white woman in York County and had four sons, besides William he had with Prossa. His later sons, William, Daniel, Christopher, and Thomas, born from his marriage to the white woman between 1655 to 1660, were described as "mulatto" in surviving records. Those branches of Mihill's family quickly became light-skinned in just a few generations. Mihill Gowen moved to Merchants Hundred Parish, adjacent to Martin's Hundred, in James City County, and received a land grant of 40 acres in 1668. Mihill died in 1708, at the age of about seventy-three.

Mihill appeared to prosper after his move and was able to purchase some land. The Barnhouse name in the next document indicates that this is the same Mihill.

"8 Feb 1668 Mihill Gowree, 30 or 40 acres situate in Mchants hundred parrish in James City County, formerly belonging to John Turner, Dec'd and by him purchased of Capt. Rich. Barnehouse and lately found to escheat...20 Dec 1666 & now granted to sd Gowree." [43] On September 11, 1717, a James City County inquisition found that "Mihil Goen late of said County of James City dyed seised of 30 or 40 acres...Escheat..." [43]

It was custom, in early Virginia, when land was "escheated," it indicated that there were no legal living heirs. Family historians argued that Mihill had descendants, but his children were not from a marriage legally recognized by the authorities. Some believed it was because he was Black. Whichever reasoning or both, Mihill's estate was denied the inheritance of land.

Mihill Gowen's children were:

> With Prossa (Rosa), he had: William, born August 25, 1655, who received a land grant in Charles City County on April 20, 1687.
>
> He may have had a son, Edward, born c1681.

# A Man of Significance

Mihill and the unknown white woman may have had:

> Daniel, born c1657, who had a patent for 100 acres in Gloucester County in 1679 and 52 acres in 1698.

> Christopher was born in c1658. He and his wife, Anne, lived in Abingdon Parish in January 1679, when their son, Michael, was born.

> Mihill also had Phillip.

> Thomas Going was born about 1660.

> James, Thomas' son, was born in 1683.

In Westmoreland County, Thomas, at the age of 37, had incurred large gambling debts. But he had a reverse of misfortune in 1707. [44]

## Chapter Thirty-One
### Third Generation: Thomas Christopher Gowen

Thomas Christopher Gowen (1660-1726) is my fifth great-grandfather and the last ancestor group identified by my Ancestry DNA results. As listed with all of Mihill's children, Thomas is Mihill's youngest son by his second wife.

It is said that Thomas raised and raced horses. A clue to that was in the previous chapter about his going in debt. It appeared that dept was accrued gambling at the races. Thomas was involved in several court cases in which he either was suing someone or someone was suing him.

At thirty-seven, he had acquired serious gambling losses and debts in Westmoreland County. He seemed to be a man who was willing to take chances. That loss was overcome in 1707 when Thomas was granted about 650 acres in Stafford County below the falls of the Potomac River, according to genealogist Paul Heinegg. [45] The land

## A Man of Significance

was directly adjacent to the property owned by Robert Alexander.

Gowen's name came up in court many years later in an unrelated case, attesting to Thomas' willingness to live life fully. "In a 1767 land dispute, a 70-year-old deponent, Charles Griffith, related a conversation which he had with Major Robert Alexander, 43 years previously in 1724. Major Robert Alexander, who owned land adjoining the Gowens, supposedly said of them: 'he had a great mind to turn the Molatto rascals (who were then his tenants) off his land.'" [46]

From the same reference, the Gowen family continued to be criticized for not spending their money wisely. It was not "quiet money," as I heard someone say about a friend.

Griffin continued, "he was at a Race in the same year where the Goings were (who then had running horses) and that the old people were talking about the Goings taking up Alexander's land and selling it to Thomas and Todd which land the old people then said was in Alexanders back line or at least the greatest part of it...and if it were not for the Alexander's land...the Goings would not be so lavish of their money of which they seemed to have plenty at that time..."

I would love to have known the family as they watched their horse approaching the last stretch, or final furlong, and their thundering animal came in first. The laughter and joyous win would have been contagious.

John, Mihill, and Thomas were amazing, full of life and energy.

## Chapter Thirty-Two
### A Little History of Jamestown's Nearby Neighbors

I am including a short description of the nearest tribe of Native Americans to Jamestown Settlement. My fifth great-grandmother was Winona "Dakota" WinuNna Gowen, a Cherokee, 1656-1740. She was born in Cherokee, North Carolina, and married Thomas Christopher Gowen in Virginia in 1671 when she was fifteen. Winona means first-born daughter, and Dakota is translated as friendly. Cherokee, North Caroline, is 445 miles from Jamestown. I found no information regarding how Winona Dakota got from North Carolina to Virginia or if her people had all relocated there. However, since she is family, I wanted to research what tribes were located near Jamestown. With

Fig. 26 Native American Dwelling

## A Man of Significance

the many years of attacks by the Powhatan tribe, their people were of interest.

Near the Jamestown settlement was the encampment of the Paspahegh, the Powhatan tribe. The Native American village consisted of cone-shaped huts of smooth, shiny reeds or straw-like material, with one door opening. The huts were carefully stitched together in horizontal layers.

The wars between the English and the Powhatan tribe continued in the tidewater section of Virginia and Southern Maryland. When the Jamestown settlement was first established and colonized in 1607, it was the first permanent English colony in the Americas. The natives called the area Tsenacomoco. Thirty separate tribes were led together under Chief Powhatan, also known as Wahunsonacock.

When the English arrived, Wahunsonacock tried to make peace through trade with the English colonists. Powhatan's people traded food for weapons and tools to butcher deer and to cut hides. The English also brought copper with them to the new world. Copper was valuable enough that Powhatan used it to pay his warriors. Natives also provided skins, hides, food, and knowledge about farming and construction, in exchange for beads and "wampum." Wampum are beads made from white and purple mollusk shells. They are still used today by some Native nations in North America for ornamental or ceremonial use. Wampum would have a significant meaning to them.

Since John Gowen arrived when the first settlers came, leaving the open spaces of Angola, Africa, behind, he might have found the Jamestown fort closed in, cramped, and restricting. Despite the possibility of "island fever," the fact it was an island, was why it was chosen. The Virginia Company chose the location because it was surrounded by water. The thinking was an island settlement would have been easier to defend. Another criterion for finding the best location for the British colonial settlement was that it wasn't inhabited. Granted, although natives had lived there in the past and did live not far away, they no longer lived within the area chartered by the Virginia Company of London.

A problem with island living was the water that surrounded it. The land where the Jamestown settlement was located was very marshy, and still is to this day. All of that water can lead to diseases such as malaria. The people of Jamestown, or James City as it was called at that time, suffered many illnesses. The 100 settlers that originally came fared badly, not just because of disease but also due to famine and the attacks of Native Americans.

As more time passed, the settlers needed to improve their skills. Finally, after terrible drought and icy cold winters, they could not provide for themselves, except for the need for food. However, growing tensions continued because the colonists pressured the natives for more help.[47]

When the English first arrived in 1607, the lives of the Natives were changed forever. Due to terrible drought, the English continually demanded food from the tribe. In addition, the English didn't understand the tribal cultural practices and demanded that the Native Americans adopt the customs and culture of the English.

# A Man of Significance

One of the first settlers at Jamestown was a twenty-seven-year-old English adventurer and explorer named John Smith. With a clear head and organizational skills, Smith directed the survival effort of the people in the settlement during the famine. He also mapped the area.

Fig. 27 Captain John Smith

I think John Gowen would have loved to travel with Smith. It would again have felt like the open freedom of home. Together, they would perform John Smith's job of drawing maps of the New England coast, from Penobscot Bay to Cape Cod.

Thankfully, John Gowen and the others aboard the slave-ship came later and missed the most dangerous time in the life of the Jamestown settlement. In the first years after the arrival of the English, the relationship between the settlers and the Native Americans was not good. The village was attacked frequently. In December 1607, just twelve years before the *White Lion* landed, while John Smith and two companions were exploring the Chickahominy River, Smith and the other two were captured by Powhatan warriors. Smith's companions were killed, but Smith was held captive.

We all know what happened next. The legend of Pocahontas was taught to us while we were very young. The fate of John Smith fell to a very young girl. Smith was released after Pocahontas, Chief Powhatan's thirteen-year-old daughter, interceded on his behalf.

Smith became president of the Jamestown Colony on September 10, 1608. He was a rigid but successful president who helped the colonists survive tough times.

Also, in 1608, an accidental fire destroyed much of the town, and hunger, disease, and Native American attacks continued. During that time, Pocahontas, acting as an emissary from her father, sometimes brought gifts of food to help the colonists. She became a friend of the settlers and learned English ways and customs.

Periodic acts of violence led to the first Anglo-Powhatan War in 1609. "Wahunsonacock and his forces began a months-long siege against Jamestown, in which all but sixty colonists died of starvation and disease. English reinforcements arrived in May 1610, allowing the colonists to launch a counterattack. Fighting continued over the next four years." Warriors were told to kill any settler who came out of the fort.

John Smith was injured in a fire in his powder bag in September 1609. As a result, he needed to return to England. Smith was no longer in the colony when the *White Lion* arrived in Virginia in 1619.

*Fig. 28 Musket Firing*

After John Smith returned to England, relations with the Powhatan Indians deteriorated. Many settlers died from famine and disease in the winter of 1609-1610. The

## A Man of Significance

people of Jamestown were nearly ready to abandon the settlement when Baron De La Warr (also known as Delaware) arrived in June of 1610. He brought supplies and rebuilt the settlement. That was the same year that John Rolfe also arrived in Jamestown. After being there only two years, Rolfe cultivated the first tobacco in Virginia.

In the spring of 1613, the English Captain Samuel Argall hoped he could negotiate a permanent peace with Chief Powhatan by taking Pocahontas hostage. At first, she was treated very badly, even giving birth to a son from attacks she endured, according to a geologist at Historic Jamestown. She was finally moved and placed under the custody of Sir Thomas Gates, the marshal of Virginia. There she was treated kindly. The marshal treated her like a guest and encouraged her to learn English ways. Pocahontas even converted to Christianity, was baptized, and given the name Lady Rebecca.

Her father, Powhatan, eventually agreed to the terms of her release. "A peace was concluded in 1614, when Wahunsonacock's daughter Pocahontas, who had been captured the previous year, converted to Christianity, and agreed to marry Englishman John Rolfe. Pocahontas' marriage to Rolfe in 1614 would have been just five years before the White Lion sailed into the bay." Violent conflicts with the tribe continued over the next four decades ending in 1646 when the Algonquian-speaking Indians were forced under English rule.

Rather than leaving Jamestown and returning to her people, however, Pocahontas stayed in the settlement due to her love for John Rolfe.

On April 5, 1614, Pocahontas and John Rolfe were married. The remains of the chancel area of the church where they were married are in the photo to the left. They had the blessing of Chief Powhatan and the governor of Virginia.

*Fig. 29 Remains of Church Chancel*

Their son, Thomas, was born the year after they were married. In 1616, John Rolfe, Pocahontas, and the baby sailed for England. While they were there, the Rolfe family stayed in the Belle Sauvage Inn. It wasn't the most glamorous place and seemed to attract London's most unwelcome society.

Still, Pocahontas was received with warmth in London. She wore modern clothes with wide lace-edged collars and fine European-style hats. The English were fascinated by the "Indian" princess from the New World.

*Fig. 30 Pocahontas statue*

Most of society treated her with respect. She was invited to several parties and theater productions, often as an honored guest. It was a whirlwind of activities. [48] It is said, King James did not approve of her marriage to John Rolfe, since she was a "princess" and he was a commoner.

In Historic Jamestown, the stature of Pocahontas was created with her in the Native American style of buckskins and barefoot.

In March of 1617, Rolfe, Pocahontas, and their son were supposed to sail back to Virginia. That didn't happen. Pocahontas died the day before they would leave. Her father died the following year.[49]

## Chapter Thirty-Three
**Points of Historic Interest in the Country of Your Ancestor's Origin**

_____
_____
_____
_____
_____
_____
_____
_____
_____
_____
_____
_____
_____Added more pages as needed.

*Holy God, you are pure, creative love. I ask that you love and bless my family: those who went before and my family now, for all those in Heaven and on earth are yours. May anything I say, think, or do, not block their view of seeing you. I thank you for them, for you know the family I need and those who need me. In the name of Jesus, your son, I pray. Amen*

Or, write your own.

_____
_____
_____
_____
_____
_____
_____
_____

Now write three things you're thankful for, because of your ancestor.

1._____
_____

2._____
_____

3._____
_____

## Chapter Thirty-Four
### Slave Laws

The Angolan-born John Gowen arrived when no one cared about race in Virginia. Mixed marriages and mixed-race children had already been happening with the English and the local native tribes with no negative societal impact. The only thing the Virginians cared about was that they were Christian. It wasn't until the 1660s, years after John and Margaret took white spouses, that slave laws were written.

**Virginia Slave Laws**

December 1662

> *Whereas* some doubts have arisen whether children got by any Englishman upon a Negro woman should be slave or free, *be it therefore enacted and declared by this present Grand Assembly,* that all children born in this country shall be held bond or free only according to the

condition of the mother; and that if any Christian shall commit fornication with a Negro man or woman, he or she so offending shall pay double the fines imposed by the former act.[50]

September 1667

*Whereas* some doubts have risen whether children that are slaves by birth, and by the charity and piety of their owners made partakers of the blessed sacrament of baptism, should by virtue of their baptism be made free, *it is enacted and declared by this Grand Assembly, and the authority thereof,* that the conferring of baptism does not alter the condition of the person as to his bondage or freedom; that diverse masters, freed from this doubt may more carefully endeavor the propagation of Christianity by permitting children, though slaves, or chose of greater growth if capable, to be admitted to that sacrament.

September 1668

*Whereas* it has been questioned whether servants running away may be punished with corporal punishment by their master or magistrate, since the act already made gives the master satisfaction by prolonging their time by service, *it is declared and enacted by this Assembly* that moderate corporal punishment inflicted by master or magistrate upon a runaway servant shall not deprive the master of the satisfaction allowed by the law, the one being as necessary to reclaim them from persisting in that idle course as the other is just to repair the damages sustained by the master.

October 1669

*Whereas* the only law in force for the punishment of refractory servants resisting their master, mistress, or over-seer cannot be inflicted upon Negroes, nor the obstinacy of many of them be suppressed by other than violent means, *be it enacted and declared by this Grand Assembly* if any slave resists his master (or other by his master's order correcting him) and by the extremity of the correction should chance to die, that his death shall not be accounted a felony, but the master (or that other person appointed by the master to punish him) be acquitted from molestation, since it cannot be presumed that premeditated malice (which alone makes murder a felony) should induce any man to destroy his own estate. [51]

## Slavery Law in Virginia - Growth of the Black Population

The population of Blacks in Virginia grew as the need for tobacco grew. Enslaved people did all the work and were a valuable asset on the farms and plantations.

| Year | Population |
|---|---|
| 1625 | 23 |
| 1648 | 300 |
| 1671 | 2000 |
| 1680 | 3,000 |
| 1700 | 16,390 |
| 1720 | 26,559 |
| 1730 | 30,000 |
| 1740 | 60,000 |

How very quickly the new world changed from a somewhat inclusive society to one of white dominance and the presence of walking shadows. Black people, present but not acknowledged, were only here to serve their owners.

## Chapter Thirty-Five
**Blessed**

John Gowen was blessed. When he was an adult, he must have known he was Blessed. People who are aware they are Blessed are positive and seek no one else to blame. They creatively make a blessing out of what comes their way each day, love and forgive their neighbors, are assertive without being aggressive, and seek to bless others out of what the Lord has given them. Doesn't that sound like John?

Forgiveness does not mean you will not hold the person accountable for what he or she has done to offend you. It means you have set them free from any anger or hate you may harbor against them. Therefore, you are also released from the midnight hours of haunting anger and pain.

If you haven't yet, find an ancestor of whom you were unaware. Use the suggestions in this book to get to know your distant relative. If you aren't into genealogy, think of someone you know who is quite different from you. Perhaps your grandfather or grandmother was from a far-distant culture. Maybe you had heard rumors of them, but no family member ever discussed their past family. You may have grown up in a Hispanic community near the Rio Grande, but your name is Jones. Your busy parents never talked much about their families. Get as much information from living relatives while you still have them with you, then get to know yourself a little more through the ones who went before.

When we lived in New Mexico, we knew a wonderful Japanese family. Their two sons were born in the United States and were typical southwestern kids. One of the boys, a New Mexico State University student, told us about an incident while walking to class one day.

A group of visitors from Japan needed help in finding their way around the large land-grant University. Currently, NMSU consists of 6,000 acres and enrolls 21,000 students from the U.S. and 71 foreign countries, as compared in size to Ohio State University, also a land-grant university, with its 1,600 acres. When the Japanese visitors saw Barry Watanabe (a fictitious name), they ran up to him, smiling, laughing, and probably asking questions about the campus. Where's the problem with that? Barry did not speak a word of Japanese. For our purposes in this book, Barry might choose one of his grandparents, whom he never met, and get to know them. He might even study the Japanese language.

Another family, with the last name Martinez, lived next door to us in Las Cruces. Mr. and Mrs. Martinez were both Hispanic, born in Mexico. Their two elementary school-age children were Americanized and spoke no Spanish. The parents had refused to let the children speak their language, hoping they would have no accent and therefore experience no discrimination. Over a cup of coffee at the kitchen table in my house, I suggested a possible fun time to Mrs. Martinez. Her family could use mealtime around the table to speak Spanish. That would separate the two languages so as not to mix them. Plus, it would be a wonderful opportunity for the children to learn a second language. Now that the children are adults, they may choose to research a family member from a culture they had never been introduced to as children.

Perhaps you are an African American who had a White planter as a distant grandfather. While the man is a grandfather, you may not have even thought of calling him Grandpa.

Not to dismiss your grandfather's participation in slavery, but to free you from anger, resentment, and perhaps a distorted self-image, I suggest you research that grandfather. Learn about his people, culture, and family's land of origin. Perhaps if you knew him, you could experience a sense of belonging to all of humankind without including the label of race. You, too, will be Blessed.

I feel so honored to be included in God's greater family. Writing John Gowen, a man of significance, on my family tree, has burst my little bubble and let me soar to the farthest point of God's created family.

## Chapter Thirty-Six
**Are You Blessed?**

Do you consider yourself Blessed? You may have found other words to describe yourself. Wonderful. Take your time. Remember, who you are is different from what you are, or what you do. Although the answer to, "What do you do?" often helps define who you are, try to describe the essence of who you truly are, and write your ideas here.

_____
_____
_____
_____

*Holy God, you are pure, creative love. I ask that you love and bless my family: those who went before and my family now, for all those in Heaven and on earth are yours. May anything I say, think, or do, not block their view of seeing you. I thank you for them, for you know the family I need and those who need me. In the name of Jesus, your son, I pray. Amen*

Doris Gaines Rapp, Ph.D.

Or, write your own.

_____
_____
_____
_____
_____
_____
_____
_____
_____

Now write three things you're thankful for, because of your ancestor.

1._____

2._____

3._____

## Chapter Thirty-Seven
### A Personality Sketch

At a time in history when Angolans were brought to the colonies in slave-ships, John Gowen made the best of his capture. He worked hard and raised the money to break his own chains and those of his son, Mihill. Some resources stated that John was the first Black man in North America to be a free man of color.

John was smart, with an uncanny ability to use the law, not only for his own benefit but for others, and even to sit in judgment over others. As a psychologist, I have often tested people's intelligence with the WAIS or one of its updates.

The WAIS is the Wechsler Adult Intelligence Scale. It tests the Verbal IQ and Performance IQ and gives a Full Scale or combined IQ. Verbal tests are Information, Comprehension, Arithmetic, Digit Span, Similarities, and Vocabulary. The Performance subtests are Picture Arrangement, Picture Completion, Block Design, Object Assemble, and Digit Symbol.

I certainly won't attempt to teach the test. For our purposes, think of John Gowen's work and accomplishments. Compare John's skills to the names of the subtests.

John would have demonstrated his abilities in Information, Comprehension, Similarities. and Vocabulary when he brought the lawsuit to free his son. Since that was a legal matter, the suit also had to pass through the courts. If John didn't write those court papers, he certainly understood them. I would not be surprised to read that he had also created the Legal papers by referring to similar documents as he prepared himself for court.

He was a very respected magistrate or Justice of the Peace. A law was written to prohibit Blacks from judging the court petitions of Whites, but it wasn't enacted until after John's death when he was no longer "on the bench." John's reasoning skills were excellent, as were demonstrated in his farming and business abilities. Even though he was an indentured servant, he could buy several acres of land to plant tobacco.

*Fig. 31 Virginia tobacco planted in mounds*

John was a hard worker, spending long hours in the fields tending to tobacco plants. He also raised hogs. Reread the titles of the Performance IQ subscales. Then read on as I describe the hands-on abilities required to grow a successful tobacco crop. Can you imagine bending over all day planting and tending to William Evans' tobacco plants? Then he arduously cleared and prepared his own acres to get ready for planting before he could stop and care for the pigs.

To understand John's hard work and other tobacco field workers, I will describe a little of the process of growing a crop. Tending to the tobacco took four months out of the year, from when the seeds were planted until the cured leaves were pressed into large 63-gallon barrels called hogshead barrels. That word is from the fifteenth century English term, "hogges hede," which is a unit of measure. The owner must plant tobacco in previously uncultivated soil, so the rest of the year was spent clearing more land. The seventeenth century was long before farmers knew anything about soil regeneration, fertilizer, or crop rotation.

In 1600s Virginia, tobacco planting started in January or February, as workers began to prepare the seedbeds. It took 40 square yards of seedbeds to plant each acre of tobacco. After the planter chose the seedbed sites, he would have the workers clear the land, burn off the debris, and hoe it to remove any clumps or bumps remaining. Before March was half over, the tiny tobacco seeds were sown. Sand was mixed with the soil to make the distribution of the seeds more equally spaced throughout the seedbeds. They then raked the beds and covered them with pine boughs to protect the tiny plants.

A month later, the plants were thinned out to four inches apart. Then the plants were transplanted in the prepared fields in May, where knee-high hills were created every three to four feet. Adults could prepare five hundred hills a day, and children could prepare far fewer hills per day. The plants had to be cultivated weekly until knee-high to prevent weeds and cutworms. Large leaves were removed near the ground and from the top of the plant to stop each plant from flowering and seeding. Throughout its growth, tobacco was subject to numerous diseases and insects.

Of all the pests in the tobacco field, the most feared was the hornworm, the same bug that attacks tomato plants. Usually, there were two periods in the summer when the worms, which grow to the size of a man's finger, were at their worst. A large infestation of worms could destroy a crop in less than a week. Planters learned to inspect each tobacco plant daily, pick off worms, and crush them underfoot.

The six to nine feet tall plants were ready to harvest by late August or early September. Since the plants didn't ripen at the same time, the field hands had to make many trips to the field before the final harvesting.

There is much more to tobacco planting, cultivating, and harvesting. John must have worked every waking hour, using his well-developed Performance skills. His hands-on Performance IQ may have been as high as his Verbal abilities. With the temperature in Jamestown around 45-49 degrees in January and February, he would have worked through very cold mornings into chilly afternoons. He was a faithful worker for Evans and a dedicated worker, achieving his personal life goals.

John would have had time to think about his son, Mihill (Michael), as he worked alone on the acres assigned to him. He may have added each copper Irish penny and halfpenny in his head as he saved money to free his son. John was a good father.

As you can see from the workload of a tobacco grower, John would have needed more time to educate Mihill himself. It would take the quiet home of a landowner to ensure the environment necessary to conduct education. I assume John was able to visit and father his son, Mihill. Their father and son time may have occurred in the late hours when the sun had set, and the tobacco grew in the moonlight.

Yes, I believe Grandpa John was smart, clever, energetic, warm, good with his hands, steadfast, and loyal. It's true; no libraries are full of volumes about John Gowen. I can only base my impressions and guesses on limited references.

I'm not saying that life was perfect for John. But there are no records of him receiving punishment or abuse while living in Jamestown. I cannot apply to John the mistreatment that happened to so many others after him. But you know the fate of millions of enslaved people that followed him.

As a psychologist, I imagine that John may have suffered occasionally from PTSD — Post Traumatic Stress Disorder. The people of Angola lived through many lifetimes of war and invasions from neighboring kingdoms.

The year before John and the other Angolans were kidnapped, there was another onslaught from Portugal. The king of Angola was exiled along with some royal family members, and other men, women, and children were kidnapped as spoils of war to be sold in the New World. We know that many military men and women have PTSD as a result of their experiences in war. John and his people lived under war, and the threat of war, their entire lives. In addition to their constant hypervigilance, John and the other captives' lives were shattered when they were torn from their families and thrown into overcrowded ships. They were sent thousands of miles from everything they knew.

Symptoms of PTSD in men may begin with:
- common physical ailments, like migraine headaches, dizziness, stomach problems, chest pain, tiredness, difficulty breathing;
- nightmares or flashbacks;
- anxiety or depression;
- withdrawal;
- avoidance;
- repression;
- emotional numbing;
- hyperarousal;
- irritability;
- guilt and shame.

As we peruse these symptoms and the causes of PTSD, it is easy to see how John Gowen could have had Post Traumatic Stress Disorder episodes. I cannot describe specific incidents in his life, as the literature does not include John's everyday experiences. However, when you read the symptoms and think of his country's exposure to war for over a hundred years before John was born, you can imagine many things that could have triggered a PTSD episode. I will not lapse into pure fiction and create a novel about Grandpa John's life. That would not be fair to him or to you.

I will refer back to the rainforest of Angola. As I researched, one of the reasons trees were cut was for medicinal purposes. The article went no further. I found no documented Angolan medications. However, my research for another novel I wrote, *Hiawassee — Child of the Meadow,* revealed many Cherokee medical remedies. I also found some research that claimed many of the native herbs actually do provide some relief from the symptoms indicated.

I would guess that John would have known what to harvest or who to contact in the neighboring Native American village, who could provide what he needed. This chapter is definitely not an ancient class in pharmacology. I know nothing about mixing herbs and own no apothecary jars. As a psychologist, I'm familiar with the medications physicians prescribe for Anxiety, Depression, and related illnesses. I'll list here a few herbs you may have heard of that the Cherokee used for medicinal purposes.[52]

Rabbit Tobacco is a non-nicotine leaf used for asthma, colds, cough, flu, and pneumonia and as a sleep aid. It grows on the prairies and in the thickets in Eastern states.

Red Clover also grew in northwest Africa, so John may have been familiar with it. It helped respiratory problems and skin inflammation like psoriasis and eczema.

Rooibos, or Red Bush, is a native plant to South Africa. It helps digestion as well as nervous tension.

Rose Hip, or Rose Haw as it is also called, has many varieties. Rose hips have been used in foods for a long time. It was used to treat cough, kidney issues, and depression.

<u>Sage</u>. We are all familiar with it in cooking, especially sage dressing at Thanksgiving. It is from the small evergreen shrub. It's a member of the mint family. Native Americans used it for its purifying energies. When they burnt sage, it was to improve balance, cleanse the body and mind of negative spirits, and connect with the spiritual realm. It was supposed to enhance intuition, improve mood and cognition, and ward off negativity and toxicity. Among its claims of cures, it was supposed to be beneficial for depression, memory loss, and Alzheimer's disease.

<u>Sassafras</u> is a small tree or shrub in eastern North America. In American folklore, the aroma of the tree was associated with healing and protection from evil influences. We enjoy sassafras tea even today.

<u>Skullcap</u>, an herb from the mint family, was used to relieve stress and support the nervous system. It was good for tension and restlessness. It was also an anti-inflammatory, sedative, and a treatment for headaches, pain, anxiety, and much more.

<u>St. John's Wort</u> was an antidepressant and antianxiety aid.

If Grandpa John continued to have lingering traumatic issues due to the nightmare he experienced during the kidnapping, there would have been some herbs and plants to ease the anxiety, depression, and related muscle tightness.

Whatever John's health, it did not interfere with him becoming all he could be. By 1650, he had left College Land, the plantation of William Evans. John remarried, but I could not find her name. She may have been a White servant since there would have been few free Black women. John's new marriage produced a second son, Philip, who, like Mihill, was indentured to guarantee his freedom.

John was able to fight for his own freedom and that of his son, Mihill. Family records indicated the fight didn't end for John and his sons. John was one of a few Africans who learned to use the English legal system to document the contractual agreements of his descendants and possessions. As a magistrate in York County, Virginia, in his later years, John judged the Europeans and Africans alike. According to sources, John Gowen (Grandpa John) died sometime between 1634 and 1714 in Tidewater, Virginia Colony. Since his youngest son was born in 1660, John would have had to have died sometime after that.

One resource listed his death as 1715 at 98 or 99. However, simple arithmetic would make John 110 years old in 1715, unlikely but possible. Whatever your guess may be, Grandpa John may have lived a long life. Besides Mihill and Philip, he may have had four additional sons.

You may have found additional, valid research about John Gowen. I would like to see your findings. I want to learn more about that extraordinary man. Some data within *A Man of Significance* may need to be corrected. Feel free to send a Facebook message to me about those inconsistencies and any new information you found. Some families have passed down stories about their distant ancestors who made the Middle Passage crossing. Please, share those stories too, especially if they touched the life of Grandpa John.

I understand that many of you are descendants of John Gowen. We are all anxious to hear additional stories. It's like learning parables from the past, tales from which to learn. I hope we all learn the love, faith, perseverance, ingenuity, steadfastness, and strength that people like John Gowen passed down to their descendants. It is inspiring.

John Gowen was an amazing man, as were your unique ancestors. A simple life is not lived by a simple person. A simple life is an organized life with no complaints and seeks no one to blame. It is a life lived to the glory of God.

To get to know your ancestor, place yourself in their life. When you truly know and begin to understand a person, you can love them more deeply. You don't need someone to say genealogy research is worthwhile to validate your experience. You are who you are, who God created you to be. You don't require others to agree with you to make it so. Quietly and confidently, go about being you.

The real truth of who you are is far beyond your home of origin. As you open yourself to the race of the Blessed and become a member of all people God created, you will begin to feel complete.

**I am of the Blessed Race: Blessed, Loved,**
**Ever Saved, Sanctified, Exquisitely Designed.**

Fig. 32 Blessed Shirt Design

## Chapter Thirty-Eight
### Your Own Significant Relative

When you are ready, create a Personality Sketch of your ancestor. Don't dwell on the negative. It will do no good. But don't delete the negative, either. Finding the mistakes is how we learn.

Have you gotten far enough out of your bubble that you can see the positive in other people? I hope you can also accept them as the family they are. Bless the Blessed.

_____
_____
_____
_____
_____
_____
_____
_____
_____
_____
_____
_____

_____
_____
_____

*Holy God, you are pure, creative love. I ask that you love and bless my family: those who went before and my family now, for all those in Heaven and on earth are yours. May anything I say, think, or do, not block their view of seeing you. I thank you for them, for you know the family I need and those who need me. In the name of Jesus, your son, I pray. Amen*
Or, write your own.

_____
_____
_____
_____

Now write three things you're thankful for, because of your ancestor.

1._____

2._____

3._____

# Reference

Rapp, Doris Gaines. *Hiawassee — Child of the Meadow.* 2014. Daniel's House Publishing. Indiana

## Sources

Page 24.[1] https://hampton.gov/DocumentCenter/View/24075/1619-Virginias-First-Africans?bidId=

Page 25.[2] Russell, John Henderson., 1913. *The Free Negro in Virginia 1619-1865.* Johns Hopkins Press, Baltimore, MD

Page 26.[3] Colonial Records of Virginia, 1619-1680, State Senate Document, Extra, 1874, pp. 21, 28; 3. C. Ballagh, White Servitude in the Colony of Virginia, p. 27 n.

Page 27.[4] https://mixedracestudies.org/?tag=angola

Page 27.[5] Dictionary.com

Page 28.[6] Brooks, R.J. Letter of Marque a House of Navigation. Escondido Times-Advocate. May 13, 2023.

Page 39.[7] Hashaw, Tim. 2001. Malungu: The African Origin of the American Melungeons. https://www.eclectica.org/v5n3/hashaw.html. Accessed 4/12/2023.

Page 39.[8] JOHN GOWEN'S DESCENDANTS: Documenting America's oldest African American Family https://www.youtube.com/watch?v=z7SJE14Ij7k

Page 69.[9] Thornton, John K. 2020. History of West Central Africa. Cambridge University Press. Cambridge, England.

Page 76.[10] Ibid.

Page 76.[11] Ibid.

Page 76.[12] Ibid.

Page 77.[13] Ibid.

Page 81.[14] https://www.metmuseum.org/toah/hd/acko/hd acko.htm

Page 81.[15] Murphy, Ric. https://www.google.com/search?q=Ric+Murphy+-+Gowen+-+YouTube&sxsrf

Page 82.[16] https://www.britannica.com/place/Angola/People

Page 86.[17] https://encyclopediavirginia.org/ entries/africans-virginias-first/

Page 87.[18] https://www.britannica.com/topic/Middle-Passage-slave-trade

Page 91.[19] ttps://ourbigescape.com/18-traditional-angola-food-recipes

Page 93.[20] https://travelfoodatlas.com/calulu-de-peixe-angola-recipe

Page 94.[21] https://iheartrecipes.com/pork-neck-bones-soul-food-recipe/

Page 96.[22] https://blackpeoplesrecipes.com/chitterlings/

Page 100.[23] https://www.worldhistory.org/Portuguese Angola/

Page 104.[24] https://unesco.org/womeninafrica/njinga-mbandi/pedagogical-unit/3

Page 106.[25] https://www.leaf.tv/articles/facts-on-clothes-in-jamestown-virginia-during-colonial-times.

Page 111.[26] https://www.climatestotravel.com/ climate/angola

Page 124.[27] https://www.britannica.com/place/Angola/People

Page 124.[28] https://www.merriam-webster.com/dictionary/vassal%20state

Page 124.[29] https://www.hatshepsut.co/kingdom-of-ndongo/

Page 129.[30] https://encyclopediavirginia.org/6678-e60ae7f 70f72981/

Page 130.[31] https://www.nps.gov/jame/learn/history culture/the-indispensible-role-of-women-at-jamestown.htm

Page 133.[32] https://www.ancestraltrackers.net/va/resources/justice-colonial-virginia.pdf

Page 134.[33] Ibid.

Page 139.[34] https://encyclopediaofarkansas.net/entries/ one-drop-rule-5365/

Page 141.[35] http://www.virtualjamestown.org/practise .html #:~:text=Whereas%20Robert%20Sweat%20hath%20begotten, church%20in%20the%20time%20ofTheir source: Source: McIlwaine, ed., *Minutes of the Council and General Court of*

*Colonial Virginia*, p. 477; see also Hening, ed., *The Statutes at Large*, 1:552.

Page 141.[36] Ibid.

Page 142.[37] http://www.virtualjamestown.org/practise. Html #:~:text=Whereas%20Robert%20Sweat%20hath%20begotten,church%20in%20the%20time%20of

Page 143.[38] Ibid.

Page 144.[39] Appiah, Anthony, Henry Louis Gates (Jr.). 2005. Africana: The Encyclopedia of the African and African American Experience. Oxford University Press. Oxford, England.

Page 144.[40] DeMarce, Virginia Easley. "The Slightly Mixt," National Genealogical Society Quarterly, March 1992, Vol. 80, No.1.

Page 145.[41] Heinegg, Paul. 2021. Free African Americans of North Carolina, Virginia, and South Carolina. Vol 1.

Page 151.[42] Colonial Williamsburg, Carter's Grove Historical Report, Block 50 Building 3. https://research.colonialwilliamsburg.org>view

Page 152.[43] Ibid.

Page 154.[44] Nelson, Beverly J. Ellison. Goin Lineage, WordPress.com. https://personalinjury lawyer dallas.files.wordpress.com/2019/05/goin-book-manuscript-indexed-including-info-on-thomas-goin-by-bev-nelson.pdf

Page 154.[45] Heinegg, Paul. 2021. *Free African Americans of North Carolina, Virginia, and South Carolina.* Vol 1.

Page 155.[46] http://www.genealogy.com/ftm/f/i/i/Michelle-K-Fitch/WEBSITE-0001/UHP-0453.html

Page 158.[47] Powhatan and his people - The Washington Post https://www.Washingtonpost.com/history

Page 162.[48] https://www.historic-uk.com/HistoryUK/HistoryofEngland/Pocahontas-In-England/

Page 163.[49] https://encyclopediavirginia.org/entries/first-anglo-powhatan-war-1609-1614/

Page 167.[50] William Waller Hening, *Statutes at Large; Being a Collection of all the Laws of Virginia* (Richmond, VA, 1809-23), Vol. 11, pp. 170, 260, 266, 270.

Page 168.[51] Ibid.

Page 181.[52] https://www.legendsofamerica.com › na-herbs

## Other Books by Doris Gaines Rapp

### Fiction

Honeysuckle Rose
The Boy with the Golden Horn
Tucker's Perfect Day
The Many Lives of Tucker McBride
Tucker McBride
Length of Days Trilogy
Just in Time
News at Eleven
Escape from the Shadows
Escape from the Belfry
Hiawassee – Child of the Meadow
Smoke from Distant Fires
Length of Days – Search for Freedom
Length of Days – Beyond the Valley of the Keepers
Length of Days – The Age of Silence

### Non-Fiction

Pray Them to Heaven

Promote Yourself

Prayer Therapy of Jesus

Waiting for Jesus in a Can't Wait World – Advent 2014

### Children's Picture Books

Shyloe and the Mayor

Lincoln's Christmas Mouse

### Registered T-Shirt Design

"I Am Blessed" design on page 185

is a copyrighted T-shirt design. A few T-shirts are available while supplies last. Check on website, www.dorisgainesrapp.com

## About the Author

Doris Gaines Rapp, Ph.D. is an author, psychologist, educator, and speaker. Her books are loved by all those who read them. Doris enjoys painting and drawing, including the covers of three of her books and the interior pages of one. She has spoken before many groups, has sung for many others, and has written songs she shares. Rapp continues to be fascinated with the many ancestors she has found through DNA testing. Their names aren't enough, however. She has started researching all she can find, starting with her seventh great-grandfather, John Gowen.

While still a full-time psychologist, Doris directed the counseling centers at Taylor University and then Bethel University. She has taught undergraduate and graduate courses in psychology at local universities. Rapp taught a graduate course in Counseling at the Caribbean Graduate School of Theology in Kingston, Jamaica.

Doris and her husband, Bill, reared six children. Now that they are grown, Doris and Bill enjoy their small-town life. She loves the stories that come to her, and Bill still serves as a pastor and Chaplin. Dr. Rapp's desire for all of you — "I hope you live all of your life."

www.ingramcontent.com/pod-product-compliance
Lightning Source LLC
Chambersburg PA
CBHW042125100526
44587CB00026B/4181